SMALL-BATCH BAKING FOR

*C*HOCOLATE *L*sOVERS

ALSO BY DEBBY MAUGANS

Small-Batch Baking
Beyond the Bowl: A Cereal Lover's Ultimate Cookbook

SMALL-BATCH BAKING FOR
Chocolate Lovers

DEBBY MAUGANS

THOMAS DUNNE BOOKS

St. Martin's Griffin

New York

THOMAS DUNNE BOOKS.
An imprint of St. Martin's Press.

SMALL-BATCH BAKING FOR CHOCOLATE LOVERS. Copyright © 2011 by Debby Maugans. All rights reserved. Printed in the United States of America. For information, address St. Martin's Press, 175 Fifth Avenue, New York, N.Y. 10010.

Food photographs by Sandra Stambaugh Photography
Book design by Phil Mazzone

www.thomasdunnebooks.com
www.stmartins.com

ISBN 978-0-312-61224-5

First Edition: February 2011

10   9   8   7   6   5   4   3   2   1

For Joe Man, who held me up first and always

CONTENTS

෧෨

SMALL-BATCH BAKING FOR

Chocolate Lovers

INTRODUCTION
Everything Is Better with Chocolate

❧

*N*early every morning, my husband, Lindsay, breaks off a tiny square of an 84-percent cacao chocolate bar and slides it into my mouth before I am fully awake. The deep chocolate flavor melting and lingering on a virgin tongue first thing in the morning is indeed a sweet sensation.

After my husband listened to an NPR radio show about chocolate tasting, with a mention of chocolatier Steve DeVries in particular, Lindsay did some investigating and learned about DeVries's travels around the world to find the perfect cacao beans for making chocolate. He ordered a sampling of DeVries chocolate bars to surprise me and, since that first luscious morning experience with chocolate, we have rarely spent a night without a bar by our bedside.

You may have deduced that I am a chocoholic. If the cake, muffin, cookie, tart, or soufflé is not chocolate, I can usually pass it up. I love looking over a restaurant menu at the crème brûlées and tortes and tarts and cakes; but if it has no chocolate in it, I am going to skip it. If I am at a bakery, the inclusion of chocolate helps me narrow down the seemingly impossible decision of which treat to buy. I cannot imagine why anyone should ever want a birthday cake that was not, at least partially, chocolate.

Basically, if it contains sugar, it has to be chocolate.

I am fortunate my passion for chocolate has appeared during my development of small-batch recipe creations. Today, there are countless, tiny 2- to 4-ounce bars of artisan chocolates available. The premium quality of chocolate can mean the difference between a *good* chocolate soufflé and a *heavenly* one. Because the recipe yields just 2 servings, all you need is a single chocolate bar to complete the recipe—so it's possible to splurge on a unique flavor palate.

For this book, I developed small batches of my favorite chocolate treats, and I have updated some previous recipes to include chocolate—even when chocolate is not native to the recipe. Take baklava, for example; I put chocolate in the nut filling, and the results were amazing. It has the same texture and honeyed syrup, but with chocolate-covered nut layers between the crisp pastry. Likewise, cinnamon rolls are more tempting when they have chocolate rolled up with the nuts and cinnamon sugar. Pumpkin pie is really something to be thankful for, too, when you add melted chocolate to the filling. And shortbread, sugar cookies, and many more are just better . . . with chocolate.

My twenty-three-year-old daughter survived her high school years largely because I made pans of small-batch brownies for her at the very first sign of teenage-girl angst. Now, armed with baking skills for tools to reduce her stress, she makes a mini loaf pan of them for herself, in her own apartment, completely assuaging whatever ails her at the time.

My eight-year-old daughter and I bake small batches of Simply the Best Chocolate Chip Cookies often, sometimes every other day, because we can eat them in under 30 minutes (start to finish), warm from the oven. We love this small-batch process; no more waiting on baking sheets to cool so you can put the next batch in the oven. (With her youthful attention span, she was always "done" with baking them after the first sheet of cookies went into the oven, anyway.)

The recipes in this book are perfect for mothers and grandmothers to bake with children. It's easy to make measuring ingredients into a terrific math lesson in fractions, weights, and measures. Baking in small batches is instant gratification; you will be eating what you bake in less time than it would take to go to the store and buy a bag of cookies—anyone who's spent time with kids knows about their restricted attention span! Perhaps most satisfying is that the process is much less messy than if you were baking a large batch. I know from experience: when a child simply has to measure ½ cup flour, there is less to clean up.

Small-batch recipes can be a great entree for aspiring cooks who want to learn to bake. My older daughter's college friends loved *Small-Batch Baking*; they learned serious baking techniques and were able to practice often. It is the perfect cookbook for someone in their first apartment; the recipes can even be baked in a good toaster oven. (My younger daughter and I once baked cookies in her Easy-Bake Oven!)

For empty nesters and people living the single, high life, this is a must-have cookbook. It will put baking back into your lives, because the recipes are scaled back to manageable proportions. There will be no leftovers to lure you into overindulging, but you may be tempted to bake a different chocolate treat every day.

Small-Batch Chocolate Baking Know-How

What You Need to Get Started—Equipment, Ingredients and

Measuring Techniques, and Storing Ingredients

❦

Many people have remarked to me, since the first *Small-Batch Baking* book, that baking is a scientific process. Well, in fact, it is but it need not be dauntingly so. True, I did graduate from Virginia Tech with a BS in home economics and had to take several chemistry courses along with the food-related; some of that knowledge from long ago nagged at me while I worked with these recipes. But what has turned me into a baker is the experimenting I have done over the years—the successes and the failures have added to that basic knowledge and have given me a "feel" for baking. Believe me, my grandmother did not take as many science courses as I did, and she was one fabulous baker. All you need to learn is a willingness to practice.

This book can give you a lot of practice, because you can bake almost every day and still not overindulge. You can hone your baking skills and not eat too much of a good thing. Following the guidelines of moderation and portion control as you treat yourself is the ultimate "having your cake and eating it all, too."

Most methods I describe in *Small-Batch Baking for Chocolate Lovers* are the same as one would use for baking large batches, i.e., you mix cookie dough the same way except in a smaller bowl with less ingredients. But it is not always possible to divide a standard recipe by halves, thirds, or quarters and arrive at the same flavor and texture. So the recipe ingredients are specifically tailored to baking small batches, and they will result in the quality of baked goods you expect from its traditional counterpart. The formulas I have worked out and the clear instructions on manipulating them will give you success and confidence in your baking skills.

EQUIPMENT

Since the original *Small-Batch Baking* was published in 2005, many manufacturers have come out with smaller pans tailored to baking in miniature. And while those can be fun and efficient, honestly, you can most likely use what is already in your kitchen. I love to recycle 8-ounce and 14- to 15-ounce cans from standard pantry items—like water chestnuts and tomatoes—for baking; they are perfectly safe to use in the oven.

For muffins and small cakes, 6-cup muffin pans with standard- and jumbo-size cups are easily found in supermarkets, kitchen shops, home goods stores, and online. Petite loaf pans, with a 2-cup capacity, are the perfect size for baking loaf breads and cakes. For tarts, I like to use 4½-inch-diameter tart pans with removable bottoms; the 4-inch-diameter tart pans are also good for baking individual pies. Both sizes have removable bottoms for easier serving. And, actually, you can make pies in jumbo muffin cups; look through the section on muffin pans to see how to do it.

At the beginning of this book's testing phase, I bought an inexpensive set of toaster oven baking equipment that included a small wire rack, baking sheet, and baking pan. Those three items were the things I used most in the kitchen: the rack for cooling and the baking sheet for cookies and cradling cake cans and tart pans. The baking pan was just right for cheesecakes and puddings that needed a water bath. You can find these pan sets at home goods stores and discount superstores.

Here is a basic equipment list for other items you will need for mixing batter or dough and baking it.

- **The small-batch bowl.** The right size for creaming butter and sugar, mixing cookie or cake batter, beating egg whites, and whipping cream is a 1½-quart bowl that is taller than it is wide. I have a collection that began with the mixing bowl that came with my mother's first stand mixer; it measures 6 inches in diameter on the top and about 3 inches in diameter on the bottom. My most recent purchase is an OXO bowl with a nonstick outer surface; its diameter is 1 inch larger than the other one, but still proportionally perfect for rounding up the small amounts of ingredients. If the bowl is too large, shallow, and wide at the top, the small amounts of ingredients tend to fly up and around the bowl instead of collecting in the center. All-Clad makes a good-quality bowl with a handle; both brands, and others, are available at kitchen supply stores, home goods stores, discount superstores, and online.

- **Handheld mixer.** Being able to control the direction of the mixer coupled with the capability of mixing at lower speeds makes the handheld mixer a more efficient choice than a stand mixer fitted with the small bowl. It works much better for creaming a few tablespoons of butter and sugar, lightening ½ cup of batter, and beating 1 egg white or ¼ cup cream.

- **Rubber spatulas.** Every little bit of an ingredient counts when you work with small batches, and a rubber spatula is the best tool for scraping out every smidgeon of melted chocolate into a batter or frosting, all of the batter into the prepared cans, or the last morsel of cookie dough to make that final cookie. An assortment of wide-to-narrow spatulas will make sure you have one for every need and task.

- **Muffin pans.** A jumbo muffin pan, with six ¾-cup-capacity cups, is just right for baking large bakery-style muffins, single-serving small cakes, quick breads, and even deep-dish pies. If you use them for pies, line the cups with aluminum foil and butter the foil so you can remove the pie from the pan more easily. A regular-size muffin pan, with six ½-cup-capacity cups, is great for baking individual smaller muffins and cupcakes.

- **Petite loaf pans.** These measure 5 × 3 inches and hold 2 cups of batter; they are the right size for baking small loaves of quick breads, cakes, brownies, and bar cookies that serve two or three. Supermarkets, discount superstores, and kitchen shops carry them.

- **Loaf pans.** Cake rolls, or roulades, are baked in 9 × 5-inch loaf pans. In a perfect world, there would be a jelly-roll pan with those dimensions and 1-inch-high sides, but the 3-inch-high larger loaf pan is a fitting substitute. When you line the loaf pan with parchment and use the paper to lift the cake layer from the pan, it rolls beautifully over a filling. It cuts crosswise into three neat slices that look like you cut them from a long, traditional cake roll.

- **Individual tart pans with removable bottoms.** Having pairs of both the 4 × 1⅜-inch and the 4½ × ¾-inch tart pans is helpful with this cookbook. The 4-inch is just the right size for making fluted crust, deep-dish pies; they will come out easily from the pan if you coat the inside of the tart pan with cooking spray before baking the crust. The wider tart pans are good to use when the filling is somewhat richer in flavor and you want a thinner layer of it.

- **Recycled cans.** This is my favorite recycling act: saving cans to bake in. Taller, two-layer cakes can be baked in 14.5- to 15-ounce cans, and single layer cakes and cheese-cakes can be baked in 8-ounce cans. So save your tomato and bean and water chestnut cans or others of the same size that do not have pop tops.

  You need to be able to cut the tops off an empty can with a "clean-cut" can opener, completely removing the entire top from the now-rounded edges of the can (which forms as the can opener does its work). Remove the can's label, and run the can through the dishwasher or wash it by hand thoroughly. Use cans that have no dents or nicks; the baked cakes will not show ridges from the sides of the cans, but dented cans will bake misshapen cakes and they may not slide as easily out of the cans.

  To prepare the cans for baking, lightly butter the insides of the cans and dust them with flour, tapping out the excess. For easy greasing, use a basting brush and a little melted butter to brush and coat the insides of the cans without having to reach with your hand into the bottom of the cans to butter them. Or coat them lightly with baking spray. Place the cans on a piece of parchment paper and trace around the circumference. Cut out circles of parchment paper to line the bottoms. The cakes will invert right out of the cans, just like they would come out of cake pans.

  When you fill the cans for baking layer cakes, the batter will only reach about one-third of the way up the sides of the cans. As they bake, they rise only about one-half to two-thirds of the way up the sides of the cans. When you remove the cakes from the cans and fill and frost them, they will be the perfect sizes for individual servings.

After testing the cakes for doneness with a toothpick, cool the cakes for 10 minutes on a wire rack, then run the tip of a narrow, sharp knife around the edges of the cakes, holding the cans with a cloth to protect your hands. The cakes will slip out easily; remove the parchment paper liners and cool them upright.

Discard the cans if you see any discoloration, otherwise they can be re-used for another baking adventure. If there is any question about their condition, put them in your recycling bin. After all, they are a cinch to replace.

- **Can opener.** To bake in cans, a "clean-cut" can opener is a must. This is one that cuts off the tops of the cans without leaving any jagged edges to tear the cakes as they are unmolded, or that will nick your hands as you prepare the cans for baking. Most sturdy crank and electric can openers perform this task, but throw out your old, dull, rusty hand-crank can opener if it does not smooth the edges as it cuts.

- **Single-serving ovenproof bowl.** These include soufflé dishes, custard cups, ramekins, and even ovenproof single-serve bowls for baking puddings and soufflés.

INGREDIENTS AND MEASURING TECHNIQUES

You can easily cut a stir-fry down to size by dividing the ingredients into halves or fourths, but you can't tinker with baking in the same manner and expect wonderful results. When reducing a baking recipe, leavening ingredients, such as eggs, baking powder, and baking soda, do not reduce proportionately. This section will explain how to accurately measure the ingredients, and also serves as a good list of ingredients to have on hand for baking the recipes in this book.

- **Eggs.** In most cookbooks and magazines, recipes use large eggs. In this book, some need only a portion of one or two eggs, so I have listed tablespoon measurements of beaten eggs in the ingredient list. Measuring partial eggs is very easy to do, or you can substitute refrigerated or thawed frozen egg substitute.

To measure out a portion of an egg to use in a recipe, crack the egg into a small bowl and use a small whisk to lightly whip the egg until it is liquefied, 30 to 45 seconds. Try not to beat additional air into the egg; it will not measure correctly when it is foamy. If you do whip air into the egg, tap the bowl on the counter a couple of times and let the egg settle down before measuring.

Tilt the bowl and pour the egg into the appropriate measuring spoon, stopping when the liquid is even with the edges. Any leftover egg can be stored in a covered container in the refrigerator for up to 1 day.

- **Chocolate.** The best way to precisely measure chocolate and white chocolate is to weigh it on a reliable kitchen scale. Inexpensive scales can be purchased in kitchen shops and discount stores. Measuring with a tablespoon measure is not always accurate; chopped and *finely* chopped chocolate packs into a tablespoon measure differently. If you do not have a scale, you should get 3 to 3½ tablespoons chopped chocolate per ounce.

  Most of the recipes in this book use only a few ounces of chocolate, so it is important to know what to do with the rest of that premium-quality bar. Chocolate picks up flavors from other foods, so wrap the leftovers well in aluminum foil, then seal the wrapped package in a zip-top plastic bag. Store it in a cool, dry place, but not in the refrigerator (unless you live in an extremely hot, humid area). If the chocolate is refrigerated, the cocoa butter separates from the solids and coats the outside of the bar as a hazy film, or "bloom." However, this does not affect the flavor of the chocolate and will disappear when the chocolate is melted.

- **Butter.** Unsalted butter produces the best flavor. Although sweet foods are enhanced with a bit of salt, you want to be able to control the flavor of salt by adding it from a shaker, not the unknown quantity in butter.

  Butter should be softened for creaming. If your butter is still cold and you attempt to beat it with a mixer, you will end up chasing the butter around the bowl with the beaters. If it is softened, it will cream and blend easily with the other ingredients. Notice I do not call for "unsalted butter, at room temperature," but "unsalted butter, softened." Many times, if the butter is actually at room temperature and is too warm, it will separate, and your baked product will not have the desired texture.

- **Dry ingredients.** There is a technique to measuring flour, cornmeal, baking powder, baking soda, cocoa powder, and other powdery ingredients, and it is especially important to measure them correctly for the small amounts of batter and dough in this book. One extra tablespoon of flour, for instance, will drastically alter the bread or dessert; and if you scoop the flour from the canister with the measuring cup, packing the flour down as you scoop, you'll end up with close to one tablespoon too much flour. Leavening ingredients should be measured in the same manner; if you pack baking powder or soda into the measuring spoon, your baked product can become overly dry or develop an off flavor.

For ingredients, such as flour, to be measured in a dry-ingredient measuring cup, place the cup on a piece of wax paper and lightly spoon the ingredient into the cup, filling it a bit over the top. Hold the flat edge of a knife against the edge of the cup and scrape it across the top to even the flour with the top lip of the cup. You can then pour the flour that has fallen onto the wax paper back into the flour canister. For baking powder and baking soda, spoon the leavening ingredient into a measuring spoon that you hold over the carton or over a piece of wax paper; scrape the flat edge of a knife over the spoon to even the ingredient with the top lip of the spoon.

STORING INGREDIENTS

When you bake in small batches, you will have unused portions of ingredients that were not needed in recipes, such as partial eggs, canned milk, candy, cream of coconut, and others. Pantry staples store easily; most dry ingredients will keep for a year in air-tight containers, but other ingredients do not age quite so well.

Here are some guidelines:

- **Flour, cornstarch, unsweetened cocoa powder.** It is not necessary to refrigerate these, but you do want to keep them in a dark place, away from heat and humidity, for them to last up to 1 year.

- **Whole-grain flours, including cornmeal.** These have natural oils that can make them turn rancid quickly, so store them in airtight containers in the refrigerator or freezer and let them come to room temperature after measuring.

- **Dry yeast.** Yeast should be frozen to keep it fresh for 6 months to a year; to be safe, check the expiration date on the package. You can use it right out of the freezer; snip the package and measure what you need, then slip the rest of the yeast, still in the package, into a zip-top freezer bag and refreeze it.

- **Milk, cream, buttermilk, cottage cheese, ricotta cheese, sour cream, yogurt.** Store these in the refrigerator and, for best quality and flavor, use by the expiration or sell by date. On the other hand, if it smells and tastes fresh, you can sometimes use it a couple of days after the date on the package.

- **Cream cheese.** Usually, cream cheese will last 2 weeks past the expiration date on the package if it is kept in the refrigerator.

- **Butter.** Leave it in the original wrapper to store in the refrigerator for 1 to 3 months. You can freeze it for up to 6 to 9 months; be sure to wrap it well in moisture-proof freezer packaging material that will prevent freezer burn as well as keep odors from other foods from leaking into the packaging and absorbing into the butter. Thaw the butter in the refrigerator.

- **Spices.** Store the jar, tightly sealed, in a cool, dark, dry place, away from appliances that produce heat. Ground spices will keep for 6 months; whole spices and dried herbs, about 1 year.

- **Sweetened flaked coconut, dried fruits, such as raisins, apricots, currants, cherries, cranberries.** Store these products in zip-top bags in a cool, dark, dry place for 6 months.

- **Jams, jellies, and preserves, such as raspberry, apricot, and blueberry.** After you open them, store them in the refrigerator for 4 to 6 months.

- **Homemade dessert sauces, such as caramel and chocolate sauce.** Store in a covered jar in the refrigerator for 1 week.

- **Peanut butter.** Although refrigeration is not necessary, it will keep for a couple of months longer than the 2 to 3 months it is good on the pantry shelf.

- **Vanilla and other flavors.** Keep the bottles tightly sealed so the volatile oils do not escape, and store in a cool, dark place for a year.

- **Nuts and seeds, such as walnuts, almonds, pecans, sesame seeds, and almond paste.** After opening, put the leftovers in airtight freezer bags or containers and, to be safe, freeze nuts and seeds; refrigerate or freeze almond paste. All three contain oils that can turn rancid if they are not kept cold and dry.

- **Canned fruits and vegetables such as pineapple, unsweetened pumpkin.** After removing what you need from the can, transfer the leftover product to a clean airtight container, zip-top freezer bag, or glass jar. Do not store in the can. Refrigerate and use within 5 to 7 days.

- **Coconut milk, sweetened condensed milk, evaporated milk.** Pour the remainder into a glass jar, cover and refrigerate up to a week.

CLASSIC INDULGENCES
Beautiful Small Cakes and Cupcakes

❧

$\mathcal{B}$aby layer cakes are the cutest of the small-batch desserts. These mini cakes are perfectly proportioned to resemble, in stature and taste, their larger counterparts; each serves one, generously, or two to share in moderation. If I were to take a picture of one of them on a dessert plate and not put a fork beside it, your sense of scale would be confused and you may not be able to tell whether it is a large layer cake or a baby cake—even if I cut a wedge out of it.

Each one has the full flavor and soft, moist crumb you expect from cake. And you can make them pretty, just as you would a full-size layer cake, with decorative piping, chocolate shavings, nuts, coconut, etc.

Which brings me to the pan issue: what do we bake these in? The answer can be found in your pantry: *cans*. For layer cakes, I use 14.5- and 15-ounce cans that have held diced tomatoes, say, or beans. One end is removed with a clean-cut can opener that leaves no ragged edges; labels are soaked off, and they are completely cleaned out and washed thoroughly. The batter is poured into the cans, filling them between one-fourth and one-third full; after baking, you simply cut the cakes in half crosswise and proceed with stacking and frosting them.

Several questions are asked of me about baking in cans, which I will answer here:

1. The baked cakes slip right out of the cans after you cool them 10 minutes on a wire rack. The cans' ridges do not hold them in; the cakes do not stick in the cans if you butter and flour them or coat the cans lightly with cooking spray. Additionally, lining the bottoms of the cans with circles of parchment or waxed paper helps keep them from acting stubborn.

2. It is safe to cook in cans. Throw them out if you see rust or nicks on them, but usually you see that only after many usages and washings.

3. Throw them in the dishwasher. When foods are canned, the foods in the cans are heated to very high temperatures. Cans will withstand the heat from the dishwasher, as well as the oven; again, just watch for rust spots or nicks after using several times.

I think that baking in cans is very crafty and a great recycling trick. I am always pleased when such a sophisticated, lovely cake is made from something I barely spent any money on.

Classic Chocolate Cake

This is the go-to chocolate cake for birthdays and other celebrations. I worked on the proportions to get them just right for a "Small-Batch Desserts for Daddy" story on www.PaulaDeen.com. It is rich, moist, and tender; with the soft ganache slathered on the layers, the cake melts in your mouth.

> Unsalted butter for greasing the cans
> ¼ cup whole milk
> 1½ tablespoons well-beaten egg
> ½ teaspoon pure vanilla extract
> ¼ cup plus 2 tablespoons all-purpose flour
> ⅓ cup plus 1 tablespoon sugar
> 3 tablespoons unsweetened cocoa powder
> ⅛ teaspoon baking powder
> ⅛ teaspoon baking soda
> ⅛ teaspoon salt
> 3 tablespoons unsalted butter, softened
> Sour Cream Chocolate Ganache (recipe follows)

Position a rack in the center of the oven and preheat oven to 350°F. Lightly butter the insides of two clean 14.5-ounce cans and lightly dust them with flour, tapping out the excess. Line the bottoms of the cans with rounds of parchment paper and set them aside. Alternatively, line 4 regular-size muffin cups with paper liners.

Whisk the milk, egg, and vanilla in a small bowl.

Combine the flour, sugar, cocoa powder, baking powder, baking soda, and salt in a fine-mesh sieve placed over a small, deep mixing bowl. Sift the dry ingredients into the bowl. Add the butter and half of the milk mixture; beat with a handheld electric mixer on low speed until the dry ingredients are moistened. Increase the speed to medium, and beat until the batter has lightened and increased in volume, about 45 seconds. Scrape down the sides of the bowl. Add the remaining milk mixture, and beat until well blended, about 20 seconds.

Scrape the batter into the prepared cans or muffin cups. Bake until a toothpick inserted in the center of one comes out clean, about 20 minutes for cupcakes and 27 to 29 minutes for cakes. Cool 10 minutes on a wire rack. Loosen the edges of cakes from cans using a small sharp knife; invert the cans and remove the cakes. Cool completely. Cut in half crosswise with a sharp knife. Frost with the Sour Cream Chocolate Ganache, between layers and on the tops and sides of the cakes, or on the tops of the cupcakes.

Makes 2 cakes or 4 cupcakes

Sour Cream Chocolate Ganache
6 ounces premium-quality milk chocolate, finely chopped
3 ounces premium-quality bittersweet or semisweet chocolate,
    finely chopped
¼ cup plus 3 tablespoons sour cream
½ teaspoon pure vanilla extract
Pinch of salt

Place the chocolates in a microwave-safe bowl. Microwave on medium power until glossy, 2 to 3 minutes; stir until smooth. Let cool; whisk in the sour cream, vanilla, and salt. Let stand until thick enough to spread.

Makes 1 cup

CHOCOLATE LACES

Place 2 or 3 ounces of chopped white or semisweet chocolate in a small microwave-safe bowl and microwave on medium power until it is soft, about 1½ minutes. Stir until the chocolate is smooth. Let it cool, then scrape it into a heavy-duty plastic bag and seal the bag. Using scissors, snip off a tiny corner of the bag to make an instant piping bag. Or scrape the cool melted chocolate into a squeeze bottle. (I get various sizes of hair color applicator bottles from hair supply stores.)

Line a baking sheet with waxed paper or parchment paper. Drizzle the chocolate in a decorative pattern covering a 2-inch square area; the chocolate should be about 1/16 inch thick. Repeat the drizzling to make an additional garnish. Place in the refrigerator until chocolate has almost hardened, about 5 minutes. Remove from the refrigerator and drizzle a second layer of chocolate on top of the first ones. Refrigerate until the garnishes are firm, about 20 minutes.

Carefully peel the paper off each garnish. Refrigerate the garnishes until you are ready to use them.

To use, stand them up on their edges in soft frosting or ganache.

Diva Milk Chocolate Layer Cake

I have one friend who will not eat dark chocolate. If it is not milk chocolate, she would rather eat a caramel. (Neither can she drink her coffee dark; she always lightens hers to beige with milk and loads it with sugar.)

This dense, yet tender cake is the one I made for her birthday, and she was completely happy. It is moist and very lightly chocolate. The icing on the cake also makes it wonderful; creamy milk chocolate buttercream meets luscious cake layers for a melt-in-your-mouth celebration.

> 1½ ounces fine-quality milk chocolate, finely chopped
> ½ tablespoon unsalted butter, plus butter for greasing the cans
> ¼ cup boiling water
> 2 tablespoons sour cream
> 1 large egg yolk
> ½ teaspoon pure vanilla extract
> ¼ cup plus 3 tablespoons all-purpose flour
> ⅓ cup sugar
> 1 tablespoon unsweetened cocoa powder
> ⅛ teaspoon baking soda
> ⅛ teaspoon salt
> Milk Chocolate Buttercream Frosting (recipe follows)

Position a rack in the center of the oven and preheat the oven to 350°F. Lightly butter the insides of two 14.5-ounce cans and lightly dust with flour, tapping out the excess. Line the bottoms of the cans with rounds of parchment paper. Place the cans on a baking sheet for easier handling and set aside.

Place the milk chocolate and the butter in a small bowl; pour the boiling water over them, and let stand for 1 minute. Stir with a whisk until smooth. Whisk in the sour cream, egg yolk, and vanilla.

Combine the flour, sugar, cocoa, baking soda, and salt in a small, deep bowl. Add the chocolate mixture, and whisk just until blended. The batter will be thin.

Scrape the batter into the prepared cans, dividing it evenly. Bake the cakes until a toothpick inserted in centers comes out clean, about 30 minutes. Let cool for 10 minutes on a wire rack.

Run a thin, sharp knife around the inside edge of each can and invert to release the cakes. Cut cake in half crosswise using a sharp knife; frost between layers and on both the tops and sides of the cakes with the Milk Chocolate Buttercream Frosting.

Makes 2 cakes

Milk Chocolate Buttercream Frosting
1½ ounces fine-quality milk chocolate
3 tablespoons unsalted butter, softened
½ teaspoon pure vanilla extract
1½ cups confectioners' sugar
1 tablespoon unsweetened cocoa powder
2 tablespoons half-and-half
Pinch of salt

Place the chocolate in a small, microwave-safe cup; microwave on medium power until soft, about 1 minute. Stir until smooth. Let cool to room temperature.

Combine the butter and cooled, melted chocolate in a small, deep mixing bowl. Beat with a handheld electric mixer on low speed until smooth and fluffy. Beat in the vanilla. Sift the confectioners' sugar and cocoa powder into the bowl; add the half-and-half, by tablespoonfuls, beating until smooth and creamy.

Makes 1¼ cups

෮෨

Red Velvet Cake

Not only is this cake a spot-on, small-batch of my ninety-five-year-old Aunt Cora's old-fashioned red velvet cake, but you can actually omit the food coloring for a just plain fabulous chocolate cake recipe.

I learned to bake during week-long vacations with her in Winter Park, Florida. I did not want to go to amusement parks; I wanted to cook. So we baked red velvet cakes and debated the issue of frosting them with cream cheese icing or traditional boiled icing. Years later on my own, I experimented with putting white chocolate into the cream cheese icing, and we now agree that this rich, creamy, fluffy, and decadent version is the best.

Unsalted butter for greasing the cans
3 tablespoons buttermilk
1½ tablespoons well-beaten egg
½ teaspoon red food coloring
½ teaspoon pure vanilla extract
¼ cup plus 2½ tablespoons all-purpose flour
⅓ cup plus 1 tablespoon sugar
1½ tablespoons unsweetened cocoa powder
⅛ teaspoon baking powder
⅛ teaspoon baking soda
⅛ teaspoon salt
2 tablespoons unsalted butter, softened
White Chocolate Cream Cheese Frosting (recipe follows)

Position a rack in the center of the oven and preheat the oven to 350°F. Lightly butter the insides of two 14.5-ounce cans and lightly dust them with flour, tapping out the excess. Line the bottoms of the cans with rounds of parchment paper. Place the cans on a baking sheet for easier handling and set aside.

Place the buttermilk, egg, food coloring, and vanilla in a bowl; whisk to blend.

Combine the flour, sugar, cocoa, baking powder, baking soda, and salt in a small, deep mixing bowl. Using a handheld electric mixer, beat on low speed to combine. Add the butter and half of the buttermilk mixture; beat on low speed until the dry ingredients are moistened. Increase the speed to medium and beat until batter has lightened and increased in volume, about 45 seconds. Scrape down the sides of the bowl. Pour in the remaining buttermilk mixture and beat on medium speed until well blended, about 20 seconds.

Scrape the batter into the prepared cans. Bake the cakes until a toothpick inserted in the centers comes out clean, about 30 minutes. Let cool 10 minutes on a wire rack.

Invert the cans and remove the cakes. Cut in half crosswise using a sharp knife; frost between the layers and on the tops and sides of the cakes with the White Chocolate Cream Cheese Frosting.

Makes 2 cakes

White Chocolate Cream Cheese Frosting
2 tablespoons heavy (whipping) cream
1 ounce white chocolate, chopped
3 ounces cream cheese, at room temperature
2 tablespoons unsalted butter, at room temperature

1½ cups confectioners' sugar
½ teaspoon pure vanilla extract

Place the cream in a small microwave-safe cup; microwave at high power until hot, about 15 to 20 seconds. Add the white chocolate; let stand 1 minute and stir until smooth. Let cool.

Beat the cream cheese and butter in a small mixing bowl on high speed using a handheld electric mixer until smooth. Add the confectioners' sugar, vanilla extract, and the melted, cooled white chocolate mixture; beat until smooth and fluffy.

Makes about 1 cup

Strawberry White Chocolate Icing

The cake of my dreams is one my college roommate's mother, Betty Miller, made for us when Sara and I went to her home in Charlton Heights, West Virginia. It was the popular strawberry cake with pudding in it, and the icing had frozen, sweetened strawberries mixed into the confectioners' sugar. Somehow hers was better than any I had tasted, and I have been on a quest ever since to duplicate that sweet berry icing. This one comes mighty close with fresh ripe juicy berries and sweet melted white chocolate that gives the icing body.

I love this on the Red Velvet Cake—it is pure light chocolate and strawberry heaven. If you have any icing left over, store it in a covered container in the refrigerator for several days. It is great to dip the Brownie Cookies (page 130) into for a chocolate-strawberry treat.

> 1 ounce fine-quality white chocolate, chopped
> ¼ cup unsalted butter, divided, softened
> ½ cup hulled and sliced fresh strawberries (about 4 medium)
> 1 cup confectioners' sugar
> ¼ teaspoon pure vanilla extract
> Pinch of salt

Place the white chocolate and 1 tablespoon of the butter in a small, microwave-safe bowl; microwave on medium power until soft, about 1½ minutes. Stir until smooth. Let cool to room temperature.

Place the strawberries, confectioners' sugar, vanilla, salt, the remaining 3 tablespoons softened butter, and the cooled white chocolate mixture in a food processor fitted with the knife blade. Process until smooth and blended, scraping down the processor bowl as necessary.

Transfer the icing to a small bowl, and refrigerate until firm enough to spread, about 1 hour.

Makes 1 cup

∾

Divine White Chocolate Layer Cake

White chocolate makes this cake supermoist. You will detect pure vanilla flavor in the cake; the white chocolate is subtle. The satiny smooth frosting really shows it off.

> 1 ounce fine-quality white chocolate, finely chopped
>
> 1 tablespoon unsalted butter, cut into pieces, plus butter for greasing the cans
>
> ¼ cup boiling water
>
> 2 tablespoons sour cream
>
> 1 large egg yolk
>
> 1 teaspoon pure vanilla extract
>
> ½ cup all-purpose flour, sifted
>
> ⅓ cup sugar
>
> ⅛ teaspoon baking soda
>
> ⅛ teaspoon salt
>
> White Chocolate Buttercream Frosting (recipe follows)
>
> Chocolate Stars (optional) (page 30)

Position a rack in the center of the oven and preheat the oven to 350°F. Lightly butter the insides of two 14.5-ounce cans and lightly dust them with flour, tapping out the excess. Line the bottoms of the cans with rounds of parchment paper. Place the cans on a baking sheet for easier handling and set aside.

Place the white chocolate and butter in a small bowl. Pour boiling water over them, and let stand 1 minute. Stir with a whisk until smooth. Whisk in the sour cream, egg yolk, and vanilla until blended.

Place the flour, sugar, baking soda, and salt in a bowl; whisk to blend. Add the sour cream mixture, and whisk just until blended and smooth.

14.5 - 15 oz can

Spoon the batter into the prepared cans, dividing it evenly. Bake the cakes until a toothpick inserted into the centers comes out clean, about 30 minutes. Let cool 10 minutes on a wire rack.

Run a thin, sharp knife around the inside edge of each can and invert to release the cakes. Place the cakes upright on the wire rack and let them cool completely.

Cut each cake in half horizontally using a sharp knife. Frost with the buttercream between layers and on tops and sides of cakes. Arrange chocolate stars on tops of cakes, if using.

Makes 2 cakes

White Chocolate Buttercream Frosting
½ stick (¼ cup) unsalted butter, softened
3 ounces fine-quality white chocolate, melted and cooled
(white chocolate should be soft but cooled)
½ teaspoon pure vanilla extract
Pinch of salt
⅔ cup confectioners' sugar

Place the butter in a small, deep mixing bowl; beat at medium speed using a handheld electric mixer until fluffy. Add the melted and cooled white chocolate, vanilla, and salt; beat at high speed until well combined. Add confectioners' sugar and beat at high speed until light and fluffy.

Makes 1 cup

CHOCOLATE STARS

When you cut out these stars with a range of cutter sizes, from hors d'oeuvre–sized small cutters (about ¾ inch diameter) to small cookie cutters, and stand several of them up in a miniature cake or tart, they turn a special dessert into a smashingly gorgeous one!

   2 ounces bittersweet or semisweet chocolate, chopped
   1 teaspoon solid vegetable shortening
   Nonstick vegetable oil spray

Line a baking sheet with aluminum foil. Place the chocolate and shortening in a small microwave-safe bowl. Microwave on medium power until soft, about $1\frac{1}{2}$ minutes; stir until smooth.

Pour onto the prepared baking sheet, and spread with the back of a spoon into a thin rectangle, about 8×6 inches. Refrigerate until firm, about 15 minutes. Using assorted sizes of star-shaped cutters, cut out stars. Place the baking sheet of stars in the refrigerator again and refrigerate until very firm, about 30 minutes. Using a small spatula, carefully transfer the stars to another foil-lined baking sheet. Refrigerate until ready to use.

CHOCOLATE CURLS

Line a petite loaf pan (2-cup capacity, 5 × 3 inches) with aluminum foil. Place 3 ounces chopped bittersweet or semisweet chocolate in a small microwave-safe bowl; microwave on medium power until soft, about 1½ minutes. Stir until the chocolate is smooth.

Pour into the foil-lined loaf pan, and tilt the pan until the chocolate spreads into an even layer. Refrigerate the chocolate until it is very firm, about 45 minutes.

Drag a vegetable peeler over the top of the chocolate to form curls. Place on a plate and refrigerate until you are ready to use them.

Texas Sheet Cake

In elementary school, my girlfriend Debbie Skinner's mother used to make Texas sheet cake from a worn newspaper recipe clipping. I remember that cake to this day . . . When I went home from school with her, her mom would have one ready and warm from the oven. It looked like thin brownies, but the taste was lighter in chocolate and a little more cakey.

The signature texture is created when warm icing is spread over the hot cake and the icing hardens. When we cut our first pieces, the icing would not quite have hardened so they were dripping with fudgy goodness. We would play for awhile and watch and wait for it to cool off and firm up, then we would head back into the kitchen for a second go-around.

That gold standard was the one by which I measured this recipe. It takes me back through her carport kitchen door in Jacksonville, Florida, into a simpler time when I was whetting my chocolate appetite.

Unsalted butter for greasing the pan
¾ ounce semisweet chocolate, chopped
1 tablespoon well-beaten egg
1 tablespoon water
½ teaspoon pure vanilla extract
3 tablespoons sugar
⅛ teaspoon baking soda
⅛ teaspoon salt

¼ cup all-purpose flour
Chocolate Icing Glaze (recipe follows)
Chopped pecans (optional)

Position a rack in the center of the oven and preheat the oven to 350°F. Lightly butter a petite loaf pan (2-cup capacity, about 5 × 3 inches), and line the bottom lengthwise and up the short ends with a strip of aluminum foil, allowing the ends to extend 1½ inches over the edges. Set the pan aside.

Place the chocolate in a small, microwave-safe bowl; microwave on medium power until soft, about 1 minute. Stir until smooth; let cool.

Measure the beaten egg into a small, deep mixing bowl. Whisk in the water and vanilla. Whisk in cooled, melted chocolate, sugar, baking soda, and salt. Stir in the flour until just smooth.

Pour the batter into the prepared loaf pan. Bake the cake until a toothpick inserted into the center comes out clean, about 17 minutes. Place on a wire rack and let cool 10 minutes.

Prepare the Chocolate Icing Glaze about 5 minutes before the cake has finished baking.

Spread the warm icing on the hot cake, and sprinkle with the pecans, if using. Let cool to room temperature, about 45 minutes; refrigerate until the icing sets, about 20 minutes. Serve at room temperature. Lift the cake out of the pan using foil handles.

Makes 3 to 4 squares

Chocolate Icing Glaze

1½ tablespoons unsalted butter

1½ tablespoons unsweetened cocoa powder

1½ tablespoons heavy (whipping) cream

½ teaspoon light corn syrup

¼ cup plus 2 tablespoons confectioners' sugar

½ teaspoon pure vanilla extract

Place the butter, cocoa, cream, and corn syrup in a medium saucepan over medium heat; cook, stirring occasionally, until smooth. Remove from heat and whisk in confectioners' sugar and vanilla. Spread immediately over cake.

Makes enough for 1 sheet cake, about ¼ cup

Chocoholic's Truffle Torte

When it is cold, this single layer of sublime chocolate cuts like a soft stick of butter or a cheesecake. It tastes like the creamiest, handmade truffle from a fine chocolate shop— luscious with deep chocolate flavor. When people first taste this, their eyebrows rise mid-bite, wondering how anything so tiny could taste so divine.

I vary the flavor with Kahlúa, Amaretto, Frangelico, and even single malt scotch in place of the brandy. To finish the tops of the cakes, dust them like you would roll a homemade truffle: put confectioners' sugar or a mix of confectioners' sugar and cocoa in a fine-mesh sieve, and sprinkle on the tops. Or sprinkle the tops of the cakes with finely chopped nuts.

For the torte
¼ cup plus 2 tablespoons sugar
2 tablespoons water
1 tablespoon brandy
2 ounces premium-quality unsweetened chocolate, finely chopped
1 ounce premium-quality semisweet chocolate, finely chopped
3½ tablespoons unsalted butter, diced
1 large egg
1 large egg yolk
Pinch of salt

For the whipped cream topping
⅓ cup cold heavy (whipping) cream
1 tablespoon confectioners' sugar
2 to 3 teaspoons brandy

Prepare the torte: Position a rack in the center of the oven and preheat the oven to 300°F. Lightly coat the insides of two 8-ounce cans (3¼ inch in diameter and 2 inches tall) with cooking spray. For each, place the cans on a piece of parchment paper and trace around the circumference. Cut out circles of parchment paper to line the bottoms. Line the bottom of each can with a circle of parchment paper; cut a 2-inch-wide strip of parchment paper to line the inside edge of the can, and press it against the inside edge. Place the cans in an 8- or 9-inch baking pan and set the pan aside.

Place the sugar and water in a small saucepan; bring to a simmer over medium heat, stirring constantly until the sugar dissolves. Remove from the heat and let cool. Stir in brandy. Set aside.

Place the chocolates in a small, microwave-safe bowl; microwave on medium power until soft, about 2 minutes. Stir until smooth. Stir in the butter pieces until smooth. Stir in the sugar syrup. Add the egg, egg yolk, and salt; stir gently with a whisk until blended, but do not beat in air bubbles.

Scrape the batter into the cans in the baking pan, dividing it evenly. Pour hot water into the baking pan to come halfway up the sides of the cans. Bake until just set, 35 minutes; the tortes will be shiny and feel firm when lightly touched.

Transfer to a wire rack to cool completely. Cover and refrigerate at least 4 hours or overnight.

Prepare the topping: Place the cream, confectioners' sugar, and brandy in a small, deep mixing bowl; beat on high speed using a handheld electric mixer until firm peaks form.

Remove the cooled cakes from the cans and remove the parchment paper. Serve on plates dusted with confectioners' sugar with the whipped cream topping.

Makes 2 cakes

∾

Chocolate Soufflé Cakes

These little deeply chocolate soufflé cakes rise and fall as you would expect, but they have more cakelike structure than true soufflés. They are light and will not fill you up, but the flavor is supremely satisfying—the perfect taste after a heavier dinner and just the right bite after a lighter summer meal.

For presentation reasons, I recommend using 3-inch baking rings, which are easily found at restaurant supply stores and online bakeware shops. The soufflé cakes slip right out of the rings onto dessert plates. If you bake them in soufflé dishes, they will not unmold; just serve them in the dishes on napkin-lined plates as you would soufflés.

4 ounces bittersweet chocolate or semisweet chocolate, chopped

2½ tablespoons unsalted butter, plus butter for preparing the rings

1 tablespoon milk or water

1 large egg, at room temperature

1 large egg yolk, at room temperature

3 tablespoons granulated sugar

1 tablespoon all-purpose flour

Unsweetened cocoa or confectioners' sugar

Mousse of your choice: Chocolate Mousse, Peanut Butter Mousse,
   Caramel Mousse (page 40)

Position a rack in the center of the oven and preheat the oven to 350°F. Cut out three 5-inch squares of heavy-duty aluminum foil and four 3-inch circles of parchment paper. Center a 3 × 1½-inch baking ring on top of each square of foil; form edges of foil up and around the baking rings, and mold to the sides of the rings to create individual baking dishes. Place the parchment paper circles in the bottoms of the "baking dishes" to line them. Brush the parchment paper–lined bottoms and sides of rings with a little melted butter and dust lightly with flour, tapping out the excess. Place the baking rings on a baking sheet for easier handling. Or lightly butter and flour two 8-ounce soufflé dishes or ramekins and place on a baking sheet. Set aside.

Place the chocolate and butter in a medium, microwave-safe bowl; microwave on medium power until softened, 1 to 1½ minutes. Stir until smooth. Whisk in the milk or water and let cool to lukewarm.

Beat the egg, egg yolk, and sugar in a small mixing bowl at high speed using a handheld electric mixer until tripled in volume, 4 to 5 minutes. Fold one-fourth of the egg mixture into the chocolate mixture to lighten it. Sift the flour over the egg mixture, and scrape the chocolate mixture into the egg mixture using a rubber spatula; fold together. Scrape the batter into the prepared baking rings.

Bake the cakes until they have pulled away from sides of baking rings and a toothpick inserted into the centers comes out clean, about 20 minutes. Remove the baking sheet from oven, and place the cakes on a wire rack to cool 10 minutes. Then loosen the inside edges of the cakes with a sharp knife, and remove the parchment paper and foil. Gently push each cake through the baking ring onto a rack or serving plates.

To serve, sift cocoa or confectioners' sugar over cakes. Spoon your choice of mousse alongside, or on top of, the cakes.

Makes 3 servings

❦

A Trio of Mousses

Each one of these mousse recipes is a dessert on its own. Just by whipping cream and adding melted chocolate, caramel sauce, or peanut butter, you have a quick, luscious topping for tarts, cakes, puddings, and other desserts. They will keep in the refrigerator up to 2 hours before serving; I have even eaten them the next day, though they are not quite as fluffy.

Chocolate Mousse

My daughter Eleni's favorite dessert, this mousse is as luscious eaten out of a bowl as it is holding cake layers together.

> ⅓ cup cold heavy (whipping) cream
> 1 tablespoon confectioners' sugar
> 1 ounce bittersweet or semisweet chocolate, melted and cooled

Place the cream and confectioners' sugar in a small, deep mixing bowl. Beat on high speed using a handheld electric mixer until firm peaks form. Scrape in the cooled, melted chocolate and beat until blended. Cover and refrigerate the mousse until ready to serve, up to 2 hours.

Makes about ½ cup

Caramel Mousse

This tastes like jet-puffed caramel, just like the texture of fluffy marshmallows. It is divine dolloped on a chocolate shake, hot chocolate, or a fudgy tart.

⅓ cup cold heavy (whipping) cream

3 tablespoons Rich Caramel Sauce (page 244) or store-bought caramel sundae topping

Place the cream in a small, deep mixing bowl. Beat on high speed using a handheld electric mixer until firm peaks form. Beat in the caramel sauce until blended. Cover and refrigerate the mousse until ready to serve, up to 2 hours.

Makes about ½ cup

Peanut Butter Mousse

I can't resist peanut butter and chocolate. Lightened with cream to a cloudlike texture, this peanut butter topping is just the right touch for chocolate soufflés, tarts, and drinks.

⅓ cup cold heavy (whipping) cream

2 tablespoons confectioners' sugar

2 tablespoons peanut butter

Place the cream and confectioners' sugar in a small, deep mixing bowl. Beat on high speed using a handheld electric mixer until firm peaks form. Scrape in the peanut butter and beat until blended. Cover and refrigerate the mousse until ready to serve, up to 2 hours.

Makes about ½ cup

᥆ᦔ

Warm Truffle Cakes with Quick Brandied Cherries

These are a few of my favorite things, and they all go together into a simple, yet spectacular dessert. This is the first thing I think to bake when local cherries start coming into our local markets. You cannot beat this dense, single layer cake for deep chocolate flavor and creamy, light texture, and the pool of brandied cherry juices are an intense complement.

¼ cup plus 1 tablespoon granulated sugar, divided
⅔ cup halved, pitted fresh sweet cherries
2 tablespoons brandy
3 ounces bittersweet chocolate, chopped
3 tablespoons unsalted butter, plus butter for greasing the ramekins
1 large egg
1 large egg yolk
½ teaspoon pure vanilla extract
Pinch of salt
1 tablespoon all-purpose flour
Whipped cream
Confectioners' sugar (optional)

Position a rack in the center of the oven and preheat the oven to 375°F. Lightly butter two 8-ounce ramekins and dust lightly with flour, tapping out the excess. Place the ramekins on a baking sheet for easier handling and set aside.

Place 2 tablespoons of the sugar and 1 tablespoon water in a small saucepan. Bring to a boil over medium heat, stirring constantly until the sugar melts. Continue boiling until it is reduced and pale golden, about 3 minutes. Remove the pan from the heat and stir in the cherries and brandy. Let cool completely.

Place the chocolate and butter in a small, microwave-safe bowl; microwave on medium power for 1¾ minutes, or until soft. Stir until melted and smooth. Let cool.

Place the egg, egg yolk, vanilla, salt, and the remaining 3 tablespoons sugar in a small, deep mixing bowl. Using a handheld electric mixer, beat the mixture on high speed until pale and thickened, about 2 minutes. Using a rubber spatula, fold in the cooled melted chocolate. Sift the flour over the mixture, and fold in just until no streaks remain.

Spoon the batter into the prepared ramekins and bake until the cakes have risen, the tops are dry, and the centers are just set, about 20 to 22 minutes. Remove the cakes from the oven and let cool on a wire rack for 5 minutes.

Loosen the edges of the cakes by running the tip of a small, sharp knife around them; unmold onto serving plates, rounded sides up. Spoon the brandied cherries and whipped cream onto the plates; dust with confectioners' sugar, if desired.

Makes 2 cakes

ᑫᓚ

Chocolate Raspberry Cake Hearts

I first developed these cute heart cakes in a Valentine dessert feature for my former hometown's *Birmingham* magazine. They are generously cut, but since the cake and mousse are so light, they do not seem as filling as they may appear. To make a splashy presentation for your true love, place the cakes on dessert plates dusted with confectioners' sugar, and decorate them with fresh raspberries.

Of course, the cakes are great any time, and to orient them for an everyday occasion, cut the cake into squares before filling and frosting them; do not trim the layer into heart shapes.

Unsalted butter for greasing the pan
¼ cup plus 1 tablespoon all-purpose flour
3 tablespoons unsweetened cocoa powder
⅛ teaspoon salt
3 large eggs, at room temperature
½ cup sugar
2 teaspoons very hot tap water
2½ tablespoons unsalted butter, melted
3 tablespoons seedless raspberry preserves
4 teaspoons Chambord or other raspberry liqueur, divided
4 ounces bittersweet chocolate, finely chopped and divided
¾ cup heavy (whipping) cream, divided
1 tablespoon light corn syrup

Position a rack in the center of the oven and preheat the oven to 400°F. Lightly butter and flour an 8-inch square cake pan. Line the bottom of the pan with parchment paper; butter and flour the paper, and set the pan aside.

Sift the flour, cocoa, and salt into a small bowl. Place the eggs, sugar, and water in a small, deep mixing bowl; beat with a handheld electric mixer until the mixture is thick and a heavy ribbon falls when the beaters are lifted, about 4 minutes. Sift half of the dry ingredients over the egg mixture; fold in gently. Sift and fold in the remaining dry ingredients. Fold in the melted butter. Do not overmix or the batter will deflate. Turn the batter into the prepared pan.

Bake the cakes until a toothpick inserted in the center comes out clean, 11 to 12 minutes. Let the cake cool in the pan on a wire rack for 10 minutes; remove from the pan and let cool completely.

Turn the cake out onto a cutting board lined with wax or parchment paper. Using a 3½-inch, heart-shaped cutter, cut out four cakes. Discard the scraps or reserve for nibbling. Stir together the preserves and 2 teaspoons of the liqueur; gently brush the tops and sides of the cakes with the mixture.

Place 2 ounces of the chopped chocolate in a small, microwave-safe bowl; microwave on medium power until the chocolate is soft, about 1½ minutes. Stir until smooth. While the chocolate is warm, beat ½ cup of the whipping cream in a small, deep mixing bowl until stiff peaks form; quickly beat in the chocolate. Immediately drop the mousse over two of the heart cakes and spread to within ½ inch of the edges. Place the remaining two heart cakes, preserves sides down, on top of mousse layers and press down gently to adhere. Smooth the sides of the cakes and refrigerate 30 minutes while preparing the glaze.

Bring the remaining ¼ cup cream and corn syrup to a boil in a small saucepan or microwave-safe bowl. Remove from the heat and add the remaining chocolate and 2 teaspoons liqueur; whisk until the chocolate mixture is smooth. Cool until the glaze is thickened but still pourable, about 15 minutes. Pour the glaze over the cakes, spreading the glaze to cover them. Chill until firm, at least 2 hours or up to 1 day.

Makes 2 cakes

Chocolate Raspberry Cake Roll

The bar for chocolate roulade was set very high, years ago, by the one Southern cooks made at Cobb Lane Tea Room in Birmingham, Alabama. The light, moist chocolate cake layer was baked in a jelly-roll pan, then slathered with whipped cream, rolled up, and sprinkled with confectioners' sugar. It was plainly divine.

I have aspired to duplicate the flavors in a small cake roll. Of course, my whipped cream filling has chocolate in it, and I have dressed it up with raspberries for color and sweet-tart flavor balance. If raspberries are not in season, just skip them and the raspberry liqueur for a simpler, but no less delicious version.

Small-batch cake rolls can look like toy food when they are whole, as a former editor for *Cooking Light* magazine once remarked; but sliced, the servings look cut from a standard-size cake roll.

> Unsalted butter for greasing the pan
> 1 large egg yolk
> ¼ cup sugar, divided
> Pinch of salt
> ½ teaspoon pure vanilla extract
> 4 tablespoons unsweetened cocoa powder, divided
> 2 teaspoons cake flour
> 2 large egg whites, at room temperature
> ⅛ teaspoon cream of tartar
> 1½ ounces fine-quality bittersweet chocolate, chopped

⅓ cup heavy (whipping) cream

1 tablespoon confectioners' sugar, plus additional for garnish

2 teaspoons Chambord or other raspberry liqueur

½ pint fresh raspberries

Position a rack in the center of the oven and preheat the oven to 350°F. Lightly butter a 9 × 5-inch loaf pan, and line the bottom of the pan lengthwise with a strip of parchment paper, allowing the edges to extend 1½ inches over the edges of the pan. Lightly butter the paper and sprinkle the sides of the pan and parchment paper with flour, tapping out the excess. Set the pan aside. Have ready a clean kitchen towel.

Place the egg yolk, 2 tablespoons of the sugar, and salt in a small, deep mixing bowl. Beat with a handheld electric mixer on high speed until the mixture is pale and has thickened, 1½ to 2 minutes; when you turn off the mixer and lift a beater, a ribbon of egg mixture should drizzle back onto the remainder in the bowl and leave a "track" that sits on the top before it sinks in. Place a fine-mesh sieve over the bowl, and sift the 1 tablespoon of cocoa powder and the flour over the egg yolk mixture. Fold in with a rubber spatula.

Wash and dry the mixer beaters thoroughly. Place the egg whites and cream of tartar in another small, deep mixing bowl. Beat at medium speed using a handheld electric mixer until foamy, about 5 seconds. Increase the speed to high; add the remaining 2 tablespoons of sugar in a slow, steady stream, beating constantly until firm peaks form.

Stir one-fourth of the egg whites into the chocolate mixture; fold the chocolate mixture into the remaining egg whites. Scrape the batter into the prepared pan, and smooth the top with a spatula. Bake the cake until a toothpick inserted in the center comes out clean, 12 to 13 minutes.

While the cake is baking, spread the clean kitchen towel on the counter and sift the 3 tablespoons cocoa powder onto an area of the towel about the size of the loaf pan. As soon as the cake has finished baking, carefully invert the pan over the cocoa-covered area of the towel and lift off the pan; peel off the parchment paper. Fold one end of the towel over a short end of the cake, and roll up the cake and towel together, beginning with the short end. Place the cake roll, seam side down, on a wire rack to cool.

Place the chopped chocolate in a small, microwave-safe bowl; microwave on medium power until soft, 1 to 1½ minutes, or until soft. Stir until smooth. Let cool to room temperature; the chocolate should be cooled but still soft.

Place the cream, confectioners' sugar, and liqueur in a small, deep mixing bowl. Beat at high speed using a handheld electric mixer until firm peaks form. Beat in the cooled, melted chocolate until blended.

When the cake has cooled, unroll it. Spread the filling on the cake to within 1 inch of the edges. Arrange the raspberries on the filling, spacing them evenly, and press them lightly into filling. Roll up the cake, using the towel to help. (Do not roll the towel into the cake.) Place the cake roll, seam side down, on a serving platter. Let the cake stand 30 minutes before slicing. Dust with confectioners' sugar just before slicing and serving.

Makes 1 cake roll; 3 slices

ᕦᕤ

Cashew Toffee Crunch Chocolate Torte

When I want dark chocolate, this layered cake is what I bake. The cake layers are dense like brownies and are the hair color I wish I still grew naturally—dark chestnut brown. There is nothing light about it, in texture or color.

Several years ago, I reviewed the book, *Death by Chocolate*, for *Southern Living* magazine. Marcel Desaulniers, master chocolate guru, developed a cashew and chocolate cake, and it was the first recipe I baked from his book. I could not resist configuring a similar one for two servings; I added toffee bits for an extra crunchy contrast between the layers.

1 ounce fine-quality semisweet chocolate, chopped

1½ ounces fine-quality unsweetened chocolate, chopped

1½ tablespoons unsalted butter, plus butter for greasing the pan

3 tablespoons all-purpose flour

⅛ teaspoon baking powder

⅛ teaspoon salt

1 large egg

¼ cup sugar

2 teaspoons heavy (whipping) cream

½ teaspoon pure vanilla extract

Ganache (recipe follows), at room temperature

½ cup dry-roasted, unsalted cashews, finely chopped

2 tablespoons toffee bits

Position a rack in the center of the oven and preheat the oven to 325°F. Lightly butter a petite loaf pan (2-cup capacity, about 5 × 3 inches); line the bottom of the pan lengthwise and up the short ends with a strip of aluminum foil, allowing the ends to extend 1½ inches above the edges. Lightly butter the foil and dust with flour, tapping out the excess. Set the pan aside.

Place the chocolates and butter in a small, microwave-safe bowl; microwave on medium power until soft, 1½ to 1¾ minutes. Stir until smooth. Let cool.

Whisk together the flour, baking powder, and salt in a small bowl. Set aside.

Place the egg, sugar, cream, and vanilla in a small, deep mixing bowl. Using a handheld electric mixer, beat on high speed until the mixture has lightened, about 30 seconds. Add the cooled, melted chocolate mixture, and beat on medium speed until blended, about 5 seconds. Fold in the flour mixture with a rubber spatula until no streaks remain. Pour the batter into the prepared loaf pan.

Bake until a toothpick inserted in the center of the cake comes out clean, about 35 minutes. Transfer to a wire rack and let cool 20 minutes; unmold the cake. Clean the loaf pan, and line it lengthwise with a piece of parchment paper or foil, extending the edges 1½ inches over the sides of the pan.

Prepare the Ganache according to the recipe directions on page 52.

Measure out ⅓ cup of the Ganache and set aside. Stir the cashews and toffee bits into the remaining ½ cup Ganache.

Cut the cake horizontally into three thin layers using a sharp knife. Place the bottom layer of the brownie cake, cut side up, in the bottom of the lined loaf pan. Using a rubber spatula, spread half of the cashew ganache mixture on the layer. Place the center cake layer on top and press down gently. Spread with the remaining cashew ganache mixture. Place the top cake layer, cut side down, on top of the cashew ganache mixture, pressing down gently. Refrigerate to set the Ganache, about 1 hour.

Using the ends of parchment paper or foil, lift the cake out of the loaf pan and place on a plate. Spread the reserved ⅓ cup of Ganache over the top and sides of the brownie cake. Garnish with the whole cashews. Refrigerate to set the Ganache, about 1 hour. Cut into slices while cold, and allow to come to room temperature before serving.

Makes 4 to 5 slices

Ganache
4 ounces premium-quality semisweet chocolate, broken into ½-ounce pieces
½ cup heavy (whipping) cream
1 tablespoon unsalted butter
1 tablespoon sugar

Place the chocolate in a medium bowl.

Place the cream, butter, and sugar in a small saucepan; bring to a simmer over medium heat, stirring until sugar melts. Remove from heat, and pour over the chocolate in the bowl. Let stand 1 minute, then stir until smooth. Let cool to room temperature.

Makes about ⅔ cup

German Chocolate Pound Cake

I took the coconut and pecan filling that distinguishes a German chocolate layer cake and baked it right on top, toasting the ingredients to make the flavor richer. The caramel layer deepens in color and flavor as it bakes, adding a praline-like top to the dense, moist, and tender cake. This pound cake is sweet but not cloying, just rich with German chocolate flavor.

1 ounce Baker's German's Sweet Chocolate, chopped
¼ cup sour cream
1 large egg
½ teaspoon pure vanilla extract
¼ cup plus 2½ tablespoons all-purpose flour
¼ cup sugar
1½ tablespoons unsweetened cocoa powder
⅛ teaspoon baking soda
⅛ teaspoon salt
3 tablespoons unsalted butter, softened
2 tablespoons sweetened flaked coconut
2 tablespoons chopped pecans
1½ tablespoons Rich Caramel Sauce (page 244), dulce de leche sauce, or caramel topping

Position a rack in the center of the oven and preheat the oven to 350°F. Lightly coat a petite loaf pan (2-cup capacity, about 5 × 3 inches) with cooking spray. Line the bottom of the pan lengthwise with a strip of parchment paper, allowing the ends to extend 1½ inches over the edges. Lightly coat the paper with cooking spray. Set the pan aside.

Place the chocolate in a small, microwave-safe bowl; microwave on medium power until soft, 1 to 1½ minutes. Stir until smooth. Stir in the sour cream. Whisk in the egg and vanilla. Set aside.

Combine the flour, sugar, cocoa, baking soda, and salt in a small, deep mixing bowl. Using a handheld electric mixer, beat at low speed to combine. Add the butter and half of the sour cream mixture; beat at low speed until the dry ingredients are moistened. Increase the speed to medium and beat until the batter has lightened and increased in volume, about 45 seconds. Scrape down the sides of the bowl. Pour in the remaining sour cream mixture and beat on medium speed until well blended, about 20 seconds.

Scrape the batter into the prepared pan and smooth the top. Sprinkle the top with the coconut and pecans; drizzle with the caramel sauce. Bake the cake until a toothpick inserted in center of cake comes out clean, about 40 minutes, covering loosely with a piece of aluminum foil after 20 minutes to prevent overbrowning.

Let the cake cool on a wire rack; lift from pan using ends of parchment paper. Serve warm or at room temperature.

Makes 1 petite loaf; 4 to 5 slices

Kahlúa Chocolate Cake

Lately I have been ordering Mocha Americanos at our local coffee shop. Consisting of espresso, hot water, and a couple of pumps of chocolate, it is thin but strong, and a nice break from the soy lattes with one pump of chocolate that I tend to drink.

This cake reminds me of that new drink passion . . . It is strong with rich chocolate and coffee flavor, but not too sweet. If you do not use the liqueur, you can substitute 2 table-spoons of strong brewed coffee and add ½ tablespoon sugar to the batter.

>   Unsalted butter for greasing the pan
>   2 tablespoons whole milk
>   2 tablespoons Kahlúa, or other coffee liqueur
>   1½ tablespoons well-beaten egg
>   ¼ cup plus 2½ tablespoons all-purpose flour
>   ¼ cup sugar
>   1½ tablespoons unsweetened cocoa powder
>   ⅛ teaspoon baking powder
>   ⅛ teaspoon salt
>   3 tablespoons unsalted butter, softened
>   Chocolate Cream Glaze (recipe follows)

Place a rack in the center of the oven and preheat the oven to 350°F. Lightly butter and flour a petite loaf pan (2-cup capacity, about 5 × 3 inches), tapping out excess, and set the pan aside.

Stir together the milk, liqueur, and beaten egg in a small bowl. Set aside.

Place the flour, sugar, cocoa powder, baking powder, and salt in a small, deep mixing bowl. With handheld electric mixer on low speed, mix the dry ingredients. Add the butter and half of the milk mixture; beat on low speed until the dry ingredients are moistened. Increase the speed to medium and beat until the batter has lightened and nearly doubled in volume, about 45 seconds. Scrape down the sides of the bowl; add the remaining milk mixture and beat 20 seconds on medium speed. Scrape down the sides of the bowl, and pour the batter into the prepared loaf pan.

Bake the cake until a toothpick inserted in the center comes out clean, about 30 minutes. Let cool on a wire rack 10 minutes. Remove the cake from the pan and let cool, upright, on the wire rack. Spread the cake with the Chocolate Cream Glaze and place on a serving plate. Serve at room temperature.

Makes 1 petite loaf; 4 to 5 slices

Chocolate Cream Glaze
2 tablespoons heavy (whipping) cream
1½ ounces bittersweet chocolate, chopped
1 tablespoon Kahlúa or strong, brewed coffee plus 1 tablespoon confectioners' sugar

Place the cream in a small, microwave-safe bowl and microwave on high power until hot, 15 to 20 seconds. Add the chocolate, stirring to submerge it in the hot cream; let stand 1 minute. Stir until smooth. Stir in the liqueur. Let cool until it reaches a glazing consistency.

Makes about ¼ cup

Mexican Chocolate Pound Cake

Ask a Southern cook what the secret is to making his/her pound cake moist and tender, and they will likely claim it is the buttermilk in the batter. Not only does buttermilk impart a pleasing tang, but it is a magical moisture agent.

The right amount of sugar helps, too. I once asked an older friend from Eutaw, Alabama, for her pound cake recipe. She gave me amounts for every ingredient (including the buttermilk) but not the sugar. No matter how many times I "guesstimated" the sugar measurement, I never duplicated the crackled crust and perfect texture of her cake. I knew she didn't tell me on purpose to protect her treasured recipe, and I didn't dare ask again.

This cake pulls together the flavors of coffee, cinnamon, and chocolate into a sweetly-spiced mocha balance. It is especially good served warm topped with a scoop of coffee ice cream and a drizzle of Rich Caramel Sauce (page 244).

Unsalted butter for greasing the pan
3 tablespoons buttermilk
½ teaspoon instant dark coffee or espresso powder
¼ teaspoon ground cinnamon
⅛ teaspoon baking soda
2½ tablespoons well-beaten egg
¾ teaspoon pure vanilla extract
⅓ cup plus 1 tablespoon all-purpose flour
⅓ cup sugar

1½ tablespoons unsweetened cocoa powder

⅛ teaspoon salt

3 tablespoons unsalted butter, softened

Position a rack in the center of the oven and preheat the oven to 350°F. Lightly butter and flour a petite loaf pan (2-cup capacity, about 5 × 3 inches), tapping out the excess. Set the pan aside.

Combine the buttermilk, coffee powder, cinnamon, and baking soda in a small bowl; stir well until the coffee dissolves. Whisk in the egg and vanilla. Set aside.

Combine the flour, sugar, cocoa, and salt in a small, deep mixing bowl. Using a handheld electric mixer, beat on low speed to combine. Add the butter and half of the buttermilk mixture; beat on low speed until the dry ingredients are moistened, about 20 seconds. Increase the speed to medium and beat until the batter has lightened and increased in volume, about 45 seconds; the mixture will be thick. Scrape down the sides of the bowl. Pour in the remaining buttermilk mixture and beat on medium speed until well blended, about 20 seconds.

Scrape the batter into the prepared pan. Bake the cake until a toothpick inserted in the center comes out clean, about 30 minutes. Let cool on a wire rack. Serve warm or at room temperature.

Makes 1 petite loaf; 4 to 5 slices

∽

Chocolate Chip Almond Cream Cakes

Ever hear of the "runner" dance? It looks like you are running in place and dancing at the same time. That is what my stepdaughter broke into after one bite of this cupcake. They resemble Italian cream cake with moist, dense texture, but this one is extra rich with white chocolate added to the batter.

They are large, so if you would like to make the smaller cupcake size, spoon the batter into regular-size muffin cups and bake them until they test done with a toothpick, about 15 minutes.

½ cup all-purpose flour

⅛ teaspoon baking powder

⅛ teaspoon salt

1 ounce fine-quality white chocolate, finely chopped

1 tablespoon unsalted butter, plus butter for greasing the muffin cups

¼ cup sugar

3 tablespoons sour cream

1 tablespoon water

1 large egg yolk

½ teaspoon pure vanilla extract

¼ teaspoon pure almond extract

3 tablespoons semisweet mini chocolate chips

2 tablespoons sweetened flaked coconut

2 tablespoons slivered almonds, toasted and finely chopped

White Chocolate Whipped Cream Frosting (recipe follows)

Position a rack in the center of the oven and preheat the oven to 350°F. Lightly butter and flour two jumbo muffin cups (1-cup capacity), tapping out the excess, or line with jumbo muffin cup liners. Set the pan aside.

Sift together the flour, baking powder, and salt into a small bowl.

Place the white chocolate and butter in a medium, microwave-safe bowl. Microwave on medium power 1 to 1½ minutes; stir until smooth. Whisk in the sugar, sour cream, water, egg yolk, vanilla, and almond extract.

Add the flour mixture to the liquid mixture all at once; stir with a spoon until just blended. Stir in the chocolate chips, coconut, and almonds. Pour the batter into the muffin cups, dividing it evenly.

Fill the empty muffin cups halfway with water to prevent them from scorching.

Bake until a toothpick inserted in the centers comes out clean, about 28 minutes. Let cool 10 minutes in the pan; remove from the pan and cool completely on a wire rack. Spread White Chocolate Whipped Cream Frosting on tops.

Makes 2 cakes

White Chocolate Whipped Cream Frosting
1½ ounces fine-quality white chocolate, chopped
1 tablespoon unsalted butter
3 tablespoons heavy (whipping) cream
½ teaspoon pure vanilla extract
¼ cup confectioners' sugar
Pinch of salt

Place the white chocolate and butter in a small, microwave-safe dish; microwave on medium power until soft, about 1 minute. Stir until smooth. Let cool to room temperature.

Place the cream and vanilla in a small, deep mixing bowl; beat on high speed using a handheld electric mixer until firm peaks form. Add the white chocolate mixture, confectioners' sugar, and salt; beat on medium-high speed until smooth and fluffy, about 45 seconds. Store leftovers in the refrigerator in a covered container.

Makes enough frosting for 2 layer cakes, about 1 cup

Chocolate Ginger Spice Cupcakes

Ginger pairs well with chocolate, adding its exotic fragrance and subtle heat. These moist cupcakes are rich with the powdered spice; they have a gingerbread flavor and are sweet with dark brown sugar. You could eat them without anything on them, but the ganache glaze that secures tiny pieces of candied ginger to their tops adds to their sophistication.

1 ounce bittersweet or semisweet chocolate, chopped

2 tablespoons whole milk

1 large egg yolk

½ teaspoon pure vanilla extract

¼ cup plus 1½ tablespoons all-purpose flour

1 tablespoon unsweetened cocoa powder

⅛ teaspoon baking soda

⅛ teaspoon salt

½ teaspoon ground ginger

Pinch of ground allspice

¼ cup firmly packed dark brown sugar

1 tablespoon unsalted butter, softened

Chocolate Glaze (recipe follows), lukewarm

2 tablespoons finely minced candied ginger for garnish

Prepare the cupcakes: Preheat the oven to 350°F. Line three regular muffin cups with paper liner, and set the pan aside.

Place the chocolate in a small, microwave-safe mixing bowl; microwave on medium power until glossy, about 1 minute. Stir until smooth. Let cool slightly. Whisk in milk, egg yolk, and vanilla.

Place the flour, cocoa powder, baking soda, salt, ginger, and allspice in a sieve; sift into a small, deep mixing bowl. Add the brown sugar, butter, and milk mixture; beat on low speed until the dry ingredients are moistened. Increase the speed to medium and beat until the mixture has lightened and slightly increased in volume, about 30 seconds. Scrape down the sides of bowl.

Spoon the batter into the prepared muffin cups, dividing it evenly. Fill empty cups in muffin pan halfway with water to prevent them from scorching. Bake the cupcakes until a toothpick inserted in center comes out clean, about 20 minutes. Transfer the pan to a wire rack and let the cupcakes cool before removing them from the pan.

Spoon the chocolate glaze evenly over the cooled cupcakes. Top the warm glaze with some finely minced candied ginger. Let cool completely.

Makes 3 cupcakes

Chocolate Glaze
2 tablespoons heavy (whipping) cream
1 ounce bittersweet or semisweet chocolate, finely chopped

Place the cream in a small, microwave-safe bowl; microwave on high power until simmering, about 15 seconds. Stir in the chocolate until it is melted. Let cool to lukewarm.

Makes 3 tablespoons

Marshmallow Cream–Filled Cupcakes

These cupcakes do not taste the same as the packaged little cakes some of us begged our moms to buy at the grocery store. But they are fashioned after them. I was one of the children who longed to find them in my lunch box, but alas, my mother would rather me have an apple. My craving for the sweet fluffy filling has not waned, however, so I made a yummy chocolate cupcake that is split and filled with a homemade marshmallow version, then topped with a soft, thick fudgy glaze.

For the cupcakes
1 ounce bittersweet chocolate, chopped
1½ tablespoons buttermilk (not nonfat), at room temperature
¼ cup sugar
1 large egg yolk
½ teaspoon pure vanilla extract
¼ cup plus 2 tablespoons all-purpose flour
½ tablespoon unsweetened cocoa powder
¼ teaspoon baking soda
¼ teaspoon salt
1 tablespoon unsalted butter, softened
Chocolate Glaze (recipe follows)

For the filling

1½ tablespoons unsalted butter, softened

2 tablespoons confectioners' sugar

½ teaspoon light corn syrup

½ teaspoon vanilla extract

Pinch of salt

3 tablespoons Marshmallow Creme, such as Kraft Jet-Puffed

Prepare the cupcakes: Preheat the oven to 350°F. Line three regular-size muffin cups with paper liners, and set the pan aside.

Place the chocolate in a small, microwave-safe bowl; microwave on medium power until soft. Stir until smooth. Let cool. Whisk in the buttermilk, sugar, egg yolk, and vanilla.

Place the flour, cocoa powder, baking soda, and salt in a small, deep mixing bowl. Using a handheld electric mixer, beat on low speed until well mixed. Add the butter and buttermilk mixture; beat at low speed until the dry ingredients are moistened. Increase the speed to medium and beat until the mixture has lightened and slightly increased in volume, about 30 seconds. Scrape down the sides of the bowl.

Spoon the batter into the muffin cups, dividing it evenly. Bake the cupcakes until a toothpick inserted in the centers comes out clean, about 20 minutes. Let the cupcakes cool in the pan on a wire rack for 10 minutes. Remove from the pan and let cool completely.

Prepare the filling: Combine the butter, confectioners' sugar, corn syrup, vanilla, and salt in a small, deep mixing bowl; beat at low speed using a handheld electric mixer until combined. Add the Marshmallow Creme, and beat on high speed until light and fluffy, about 3 minutes. Place in refrigerator until thick enough to spread, about 20 minutes.

To assemble, cut the cupcakes in half crosswise using a sharp knife and spoon filling on bottom halves. Replace the tops. Drizzle the cupcakes with glaze. Serve immediately, or refrigerate in an airtight container up to 1 day.

Makes 3 cupcakes

Chocolate Glaze
2 tablespoons heavy (whipping) cream
1 teaspoon light corn syrup
¼ cup semisweet chocolate chips

Place the cream and corn syrup in a small, microwave-safe bowl; microwave on high power until hot, about 25 seconds. Add the chocolate chips, and stir until melted. Let the glaze stand at room temperature until thick, about 30 minutes.

Makes ¼ cup

Coconut White Chocolate Cupcakes

Cream of coconut adds the powerful flavor in these cupcakes. You will need to mix it well before you use it because the coconut oils separate during shelf storage in the can. I like to pour it into a jar or bowl and stir it well, then store it in the refrigerator in a covered container for up to a month or two. Several recipes in this book use it, so you will have it when you need it.

The white chocolate adds extra richness to the flavor and texture of the cupcakes and the frosting.

1 ounce fine-quality white chocolate, chopped

3 tablespoons well-stirred, canned cream of coconut
  (such as Coco Lopez)

2 tablespoons sugar

2 tablespoons sour cream

1 tablespoon water

1 tablespoon well-beaten egg

½ to ¾ teaspoon coconut extract, divided

¼ teaspoon pure vanilla extract

½ cup plus 2 tablespoons all-purpose flour

⅛ teaspoon baking soda

⅛ teaspoon salt

1 recipe White Chocolate Buttercream Frosting (page 29)

Sweetened flaked coconut or grated white
  chocolate

Prepare the cupcakes: Position a rack in center of oven and preheat the oven to 350°F. Line four regular-size muffin cups with paper liners and set the pan aside.

Place the white chocolate in a medium, microwave-safe bowl; microwave on medium power until the white chocolate is soft, about 1½ minutes. Whisk in the cream of coconut, sugar, sour cream, water, beaten egg, ¼ teaspoon coconut extract, and vanilla.

Place the flour, baking soda, and salt in a wire mesh sieve; sift over the liquid ingredients. Whisk to blend.

Spoon the batter into the baking cups, dividing it evenly among them. Fill the empty muffin cups halfway with water to prevent them from scorching. Bake the cupcakes until a toothpick inserted in the center of one comes out clean, about 17 minutes.

Remove the pan from oven and carefully pour off the water. Let the cupcakes cool in the pan on a wire rack for 10 minutes; remove from the pan and let cool completely.

Prepare the White Chocolate Buttercream according to the recipe directions, adding ¼ to ½ teaspoon coconut extract to taste. Frost the tops of the cooled cupcakes.

Makes 4 cupcakes

Caramelized Banana Boston Cream Cupcakes

You may know that Boston Cream Pie is not a pie at all. It is a two-layer cake with vanilla pudding filling and a chocolate glaze that drapes the cake. Since I associate pudding with bananas, I added caramelized banana slices to the filling and as a garnish for the top, and I think you will agree the change is rather tasty.

You will need a knife and fork to eat these cupcakes. You can make the cupcakes up to a day ahead; prepare the filling several hours before serving and refrigerate it separately. (Reserve the caramelized banana garnish on a plate, and let them stand at room temperature, lightly covered.) Just before you plan to serve them, make the glaze, and split and fill the cupcakes. Spoon the warm glaze on the cupcake stacks when you serve them. The cold pudding and warm glaze is a nice contrast in temperatures for the tender cake.

For the cupcakes
3 tablespoons whole milk
1 large egg yolk
½ teaspoon pure vanilla extract
¼ cup plus 2 tablespoons all-purpose flour
¼ cup sugar
⅛ teaspoon baking powder
⅛ teaspoon salt
2 tablespoons unsalted butter, softened

For the bananas and filling
1 tablespoon unsalted butter
1 small firm, ripe banana, sliced ½-inch thick
1½ tablespoons packed light brown sugar
One 4-ounce container prepared vanilla pudding

Position a rack in the center of the oven and preheat the oven to 350°F. Line two large muffin cups with paper liners and set the pan aside.

Mix together the milk, egg yolk, and vanilla in a small cup with a fork or small whisk.

Combine the flour, sugar, baking powder, and salt in a small, deep mixing bowl; beat on low speed using a handheld electric mixer just to blend. Add the butter and milk mixture; beat on low speed until the dry ingredients are moistened. Increase the speed to medium and beat until the mixture has lightened and slightly increased in volume, about 30 seconds. Scrape down the sides of the bowl.

Spoon the batter into the prepared muffin cups, dividing it evenly. Fill the empty muffin pan cups halfway with water to prevent them from scorching. Bake the cupcakes until a toothpick inserted in the center of each cake comes out clean, 22 to 25 minutes. Let cool completely on a wire rack. Remove the cupcakes from the liners and cut in half crosswise using a sharp knife.

Prepare the caramelized bananas: Melt the butter in a small, heavy skillet over medium-high heat; add the bananas in a single layer, and sprinkle with brown sugar. Cook the bananas, gently turning once and shaking the skillet occasionally, until caramelized and the sugar is golden brown, 3 to 4 minutes.

Remove six banana slices from the skillet and set aside on a plate for garnish. Gently stir the pudding into the skillet, scraping to loosen any clinging particles. Transfer to a bowl and refrigerate.

To assemble the cupcakes, place the bottom halves on serving plates; spoon the pudding mixture on them, dividing it evenly. Replace the tops. Spoon on the warm Thick Chocolate Glaze, allowing it to drip down sides unevenly. Decorate the tops of the cupcakes with the reserved caramelized banana slices.

Makes 2 cakes

Thick Chocolate Glaze
2 tablespoons heavy (whipping) cream
1 teaspoon light corn syrup
½ cup semisweet chocolate chips

Combine the cream and corn syrup in a small, microwave-safe bowl; microwave on high power until simmering, about 25 seconds. Add the chocolate, pressing it to submerge. Let stand 1 minute, then stir until smooth. Serve warm.

Makes about ⅓ cup

Chock-Full of Chocolate Mini Bundt Cakes

My mom used to make a sour cream coffee cake in a Bundt pan that had a layer of brown sugar and cinnamon and chocolate chips on the top and bottom and in the center. This cake tastes like hers did, but mine has more chocolate per bite and a luscious ribbon of caramel sauce running through it.

> Unsalted butter for greasing the molds
> 3 tablespoons sour cream
> 1½ tablespoons well-beaten egg
> ¾ teaspoon pure vanilla extract
> ⅛ teaspoon baking soda
> ½ cup all-purpose flour
> ⅓ cup sugar
> ⅛ teaspoon salt
> 2 tablespoons unsalted butter, softened
> 2 teaspoons Rich Caramel Sauce (page 244), dulce de leche sauce,
>   or thick caramel sauce
> 3 tablespoons semisweet chocolate chips
> 2 tablespoons semisweet chocolate chips, melted

Position a rack in center of the oven and preheat the oven to 350°F. Lightly butter and flour two mini Bundt cake molds, tapping out the excess. Set aside.

Combine the sour cream, egg, and vanilla in a small bowl; stir well. Stir in baking soda with a wire whisk until smooth and blended.

Combine the flour, sugar, and salt in a small, deep mixing bowl. Using a handheld electric mixer, beat on low speed until blended. Add the butter and sour cream mixture; beat on low speed until the dry ingredients are moistened. Increase the speed to medium and beat until the mixture has somewhat lightened and increased in volume, about 45 seconds. The mixture will be thick.

Using a small spoon, spoon half of batter evenly into prepared Bundt cake molds. Drizzle half the Rich Caramel Sauce on the batter, dividing it evenly. Sprinkle with 3 tablespoons chocolate chips, dividing it evenly. Spoon the remaining batter on top, dividing it evenly.

Bake until a toothpick inserted in the centers comes out clean, 24 to 25 minutes. Let cool in pan on a wire rack 10 minutes; unmold the cakes. Let cool, upright, to room temperature.

Drizzle with the melted chocolate.

Makes 2 cakes

THE UPPERCRUST
Pies, Tarts, and Cheesecakes

∽

The first chocolate pie I ever ate was my dad's favorite: chocolate cream meringue pie. I remember thinking, as I forked through homemade clouds of puffy meringue, soft chocolate pudding, and a flaky, crisp crust—with plenty of padding around the top rim—that if one went to all that trouble to make meringue and one's own pudding, one could not get away with using a frozen or refrigerated pie crust. That pie shaped my pie crust standards, and I have never served pie without a homemade crust. Tarts, neither.

Pie crust is not hard to make, especially a small-batch one. You are more likely to have success with these. You work with only small amounts; in fact, cutting the butter into the flour for these miniature pies takes less time than for larger ones, so the butter stays chilled, thereby ensuring a flakier baked pastry.

In this chapter, the pies and tarts are made from one of three basic recipes. I have matched them to the fillings: For instance, the recipe for Basic Pastry (page 118) produces a tender crust for sweet, creamy fillings that need a salt/savory crust balance for flavor. If the pies or tarts have thicker, heavier fillings, which call for crust that is sturdier, then they are made with the Basic Sweet Pastry recipe (page 120). Pies and tarts that would benefit from cookielike crusts—that are still flaky and tender—are baked in Rich Sweet Pastry (page 122) shells.

There is a chocolate pie in here for all tastes and occasions!

Salted Chocolate Caramel Tarts

Here is the crème de la crème . . . A lovely, chewy caramel layer is nestled in a tender homemade pastry under a creamy rich ganache. A light sprinkling of imported Maldon sea salt, with its soft white crystals and clean salt flavor, enhances the flavors of both the chocolate and the caramel and takes the edge off the sugar so it will not taste cloying.

For the caramel filling

3 tablespoons heavy (whipping) cream

2 teaspoons unsalted butter

¼ cup sugar

1 tablespoon water

1 tablespoon light corn syrup

1 teaspoon pure vanilla extract

2 partially baked Rich Sweet Pastry shells (page 122), baked in
    4½ × ¾-inch tart pans with removable bottoms, still in the pans
¼ cup coarsely chopped and toasted hazelnuts, macadamia nuts,
    or almonds

For the ganache

3 tablespoons heavy (whipping) cream

1 teaspoon light corn syrup

1½ ounces bittersweet chocolate, chopped

1 tablespoon hot water

Maldon sea salt crystals or other coarse sea salt for garnish

Prepare the filling: Place the cream and butter in a small, microwave-safe bowl; microwave on high power until simmering, about 15 seconds. Place the sugar, water, and corn syrup in a small, heavy saucepan; bring to a boil, stirring until the sugar melts. Boil, uncovered, until the mixture is caramel-colored. Remove from heat and immediately whisk in the hot cream mixture with a long-handled whisk. (Mixture will splatter; pour hot cream mixture in slowly.) Whisk in the vanilla. Pour into the pastry shells. Sprinkle with the nuts, dividing them evenly between the two tarts. Let cool completely in the refrigerator.

Prepare the ganache: Place the cream and corn syrup in a small microwave-safe bowl; microwave on high power until simmering, about 25 seconds. Stir in the chocolate until smooth. Stir in the hot water until blended. Pour over caramel in tarts, dividing evenly. Let stand until the chocolate is set, about 1 hour. Sprinkle lightly with coarse Maldon or other sea salt.

Makes 2 tarts

Talisker Fudge Tarts with Hazelnut Cookie Crusts

In the summer of 2009, I attended the Seasonal School of Culinary Arts at Warren Wilson College in Swannanoa, North Carolina. Each day was devoted to learning about cooking in France, Italy, Mexico, Greece, and India.

The most awesome event of the week for me was the finale: students turned the tables and cooked for the teaching chefs. On Friday afternoon, wine still poured as we ended our final noon repast together and, instead of afternoon siestas, began planning dinner strategies.

My team did dessert: a Talisker truffle tart with a hazelnut shortbread crust, a drizzle of Talisker crème anglaise, and garden raspberries. My husband had taken guitar lessons during the concurrent Celtic music week of the Swannanoa Gathering (also on campus) and had with him a few single malts to share with visiting musicians. So although Scotland was not on our list of countries to learn about, we added a few wee drams to the tart, toasting an amazing week of music, fine food, and new friends.

> Unsalted butter for greasing the tart pans
> ¼ cup hazelnuts, toasted, skins removed (see page 156)
> ¼ cup all-purpose flour
> ¼ cup plus 3 tablespoons confectioners' sugar
> 2 tablespoons unsalted butter, softened
> 2 ounces fine-quality bittersweet chocolate, chopped

3 tablespoons heavy (whipping) cream
2 tablespoons Talisker or other single-malt scotch
Pinch of salt
2 large egg yolks
Talisker Crème Anglaise (recipe follows)

Position a rack in center of the oven and preheat the oven to 375°F. Lightly butter two 4½ × ¾-inch tart pans; place them on a baking sheet for easier handling and set aside.

Place the hazelnuts, flour, and ¼ cup of the confectioners' sugar in a food processor fitted with the knife blade; process until nuts are finely ground, about 15 seconds. Add the softened butter, and pulse until well combined, about 7 pulses. Press into bottoms of the tart pans, dividing it evenly. Bake the tart crusts until beginning to brown, 7 to 9 minutes. Remove from oven, and maintain the oven temperature.

Meanwhile, prepare the chocolate filling: Place the chocolate in a medium bowl. Place the cream and scotch in a small, heavy saucepan; bring to a simmer and pour over the chocolate in the bowl. Let it stand 1 minute, then stir until the chocolate is melted and smooth. Whisk in the 3 tablespoons confectioners' sugar, salt, and egg yolks. Pour into the center of the crusts, dividing it evenly; the filling will spread to just within the edges without flowing to the edges of the tart pans. Return the tarts to the oven and continue baking until chocolate mixture is puffed and set, about 12 to 15 minutes. Let them cool completely. Refrigerate until chilled, about 2 hours.

To serve, remove the tarts from the pans and place on serving plates. Drizzle with Talisker Crème Anglaise.

Makes 2 tarts

Talisker Crème Anglaise

¼ cup half-and-half
1 large egg yolk
1 tablespoon sugar
1 tablespoon Talisker or other single malt scotch
Pinch of salt

Place the half-and-half in a small saucepan; bring to a boil and remove from the heat. Meanwhile, place the egg yolk, sugar, scotch, and salt in a small bowl and whisk until the mixture is thick and pale.

Whisk about half of the hot half-and-half into the egg yolk mixture; then pour that back into the saucepan, whisking as you pour. Cook over medium heat, stirring constantly with a wooden spoon, until the mixture heavily coats the back of the spoon, about 2 minutes. Do not overcook. Remove the saucepan from the heat.

Place a fine-mesh sieve over a small bowl, and strain the sauce through it. Serve warm or chilled.

Makes about ¼ cup

Black-Bottomed Maple Cashew Pies

I am a cashew nut. And I adore old-fashioned pecan pies with buttery sweet filling and crisp, sugary nutty toppings. So I thought, why not switch out the two and introduce a new flavor? Here is the result of that experiment. The maple syrup, reduced to make it sweeter and thicker, adds a depth of flavor that corn syrup cannot; and the chocolate layer ties it all up in a nice little pie package.

2 partially baked Basic Pastry shells (page 118), baked in 4 × 1⅜-inch tart pans
   with removable bottoms, still in the pans
½ cup maple syrup
1½ tablespoons unsalted butter
1½ tablespoons firmly packed dark brown sugar
1½ tablespoons heavy (whipping) cream
2 tablespoons well-beaten egg
1 ounce fine-quality bittersweet chocolate, finely chopped
⅓ cup chopped unsalted roasted cashews
Maple Ice Cream (recipe follows)

Position a rack in the center of the oven and preheat the oven to 350°F. Place the tart pans on a baking sheet for easier handling and set aside.

Pour the maple syrup in a small saucepan. Bring to a boil and continue to boil until the syrup reduces to ⅓ cup. Carefully measure out 1 tablespoon of the reduced syrup, and pour it into a bowl; set it aside for making the Maple Ice Cream.

Add the butter and brown sugar to the syrup in the saucepan, and whisk them to blend well. Whisk in the cream. Let it cool slightly. Place the well-beaten egg in a small bowl; whisk in a little of the hot maple mixture. Whisk the egg mixture into the remaining hot maple mixture. Set aside.

Sprinkle the chopped chocolate into the bottoms of the pastry shells, dividing it evenly. Place the tart pans in the oven to soften the chocolate, about 2 minutes. Remove from the oven and spread the melted chocolate on the bottoms of the tart shells with the back of a spoon. Top with the cashews. Pour the maple filling over the cashew layer, dividing it evenly. Bake until the edges of the tarts are slightly puffed and the centers are soft but set, about 30 minutes.

Remove the baking sheet from the oven and transfer the tarts to a wire rack. Let the tart shells stand until they are cool enough to handle, then remove them from the tart pans. Serve them warm or at room temperature with whipped cream or Maple Ice Cream.

Makes 2 tarts

Maple Ice Cream
Reserved 1 tablespoon reduced maple syrup
1 cup vanilla ice cream, softened

Stir together the syrup and ice cream; spread in a loaf pan and freeze.

Makes 2 servings

Chocolate-Covered Cherry Almond Tarts

Sweet almond pastry cream lines the pastry shells for these tarts; fresh cherry halves are arranged on the baked filling and drizzled all over with chocolate ganache glaze. They are luscious and are the perfect summer fruit and chocolate tarts.

Here is a cherry-pitting tip: If you do not have a cherry pitter, you can remove the pit with a clean paper clip. Dig an end of the clip into the stem end of the cherry, hooking it around the pit to lift it out.

> 2 partially-baked Basic Sweet Pastry shells (page 120), baked in 4½ × ¾-inch
>   tart pans with removable bottoms, still in the pan
> ¼ cup slivered almonds
> 3 tablespoons sugar
> 1½ tablespoons unsalted butter, softened
> 1½ tablespoons well-beaten egg or egg substitute
> 2 teaspoons all-purpose flour
> 8 to 10 pitted fresh sweet cherries, halved
> 3 tablespoons heavy (whipping) cream
> 1 ounce fine-quality semisweet chocolate, chopped
> 2 teaspoons unsalted butter

Position a rack in the center of the oven and preheat the oven to 375°F. Place the tart pans on a baking sheet for easier handling and set aside.

Place the almonds in a food processor and process until they are finely ground, about 15 seconds. Add the sugar, and process until well combined, about 5 seconds. Add the butter, beaten egg, and flour; pulse until the mixture is well blended, 5 to 6 pulses. Spread the almond cream over the bottoms of the pastry shells, dividing it evenly between them.

Bake until the almond cream is beginning to brown and is slightly puffed, about 20 minutes. Remove from the oven and transfer the tarts to a wire rack. Carefully arrange cherries on warm filling, and let it cool completely.

Place the cream in a small, microwave-safe bowl; microwave on high power until simmering, about 30 seconds. Add the chopped chocolate and butter to the bowl, and stir until the mixture is melted and smooth.

Drizzle the chocolate mixture over the cherries and filling. Let the tarts stand until the chocolate sets, about 1 hour.

Makes 2 tarts

German Chocolate Meringue Pies

Although there is no German's Sweet Chocolate in these pies, they taste mildly chocolate and sweet like the bar my mom used in her cakes. The custard is creamy smooth but textured with coconut and pecans in it, and the meringue is high and fluffy, just like you want it to be. The meringue is spread on the hot filling, which begins to cook the meringue even before it is put into the oven, ensuring that the meringue cooks evenly and does not weep.

2 fully baked Basic Pastry shells (page 118), baked in 4 × 1⅜-inch tart pans
    with removable bottoms, still in the pans, or in two jumbo muffin cups
3½ tablespoons sugar
1½ teaspoons unsweetened cocoa powder
1 teaspoon all-purpose flour
¼ cup evaporated milk
1 teaspoon pure vanilla extract
1 tablespoon well-beaten egg
¼ cup flaked coconut, toasted
3 tablespoons chopped pecans

For meringue
2 large egg whites, at room temperature
⅛ teaspoon cream of tartar
¼ teaspoon pure vanilla extract
Pinch of salt
2 tablespoons sugar

Position a rack in the center of the oven and preheat the oven to 325°F. Place the tart pans on a baking sheet for easier handling and set aside.

Place the sugar, cocoa powder, and flour in a bowl; whisk in the evaporated milk and vanilla. Whisk in the egg until well blended. Stir in 3 tablespoons of the coconut and the pecans. Pour into the pastry shells.

Bake until the filling is set, about 25 minutes. Remove from oven and increase the oven temperature to 400°F.

While the pies bake, make the meringue: Place the egg whites in a small, deep mixing bowl and beat with a handheld electric mixer on medium speed until they are foamy. Add the cream of tartar, vanilla, and salt; increase the mixer speed to high and beat until soft peaks form. With the mixer running on high speed, slowly pour in the sugar and beat until stiff, glossy peaks form.

Mound the meringue over the pie fillings while they are hot, making sure to seal the meringue to the edges of the pastry. Sprinkle with the remaining 1 tablespoon coconut. Bake the pies until the meringue is golden brown, 3 to 5 minutes. Remove from the oven and transfer the pans to a wire rack. Let cool completely away from drafts. Remove the pies from the pans before serving.

Makes 2 pies

STRAWBERRY CRÈME ANGLAISE

this berry cream sauce was a happy accident. I had sliced some strawberries for a forgotten dish, and found them the next day in the back of the refrigerator. Not wishing to waste them, and knowing I was going to make a crème anglaise for a chocolate tart, I threw them into the sauce. It is so good, I figured I needed to give you the option of making it, too, and spooning it over your choice of chocolate tart or cake.

> 1 cup sliced fresh strawberries
> 1/4 cup half-and-half
> 1 1/2 large egg yolks
> 2 tablespoons sugar
> 1/2 teaspoon pure vanilla extract

Fill a medium bowl with ice and water, and set it aside.

Process the strawberries in a blender container until very smooth. You should have 1/2 cup puree. Pour into a small, heavy saucepan; bring to a boil. Boil, uncovered, until the puree is reduced to 1/4 cup, 8 to 10 minutes. Strain through a fine-mesh sieve into a small bowl. Return to the saucepan; add the half-and-half and cook until hot.

Meanwhile, whisk the egg yolks and sugar in a small bowl.

Whisk about half of the hot half-and-half mixture into the egg yolk mixture; then pour the mixture back into the saucepan, whisking as you pour. Cook over medium-low heat, stirring constantly, until the mixture heavily coats the back of a wooden spoon, about 2 minutes. Do not boil. Remove the saucepan from the heat. Return the sauce to the small bowl.

Put the small bowl in the bowl of ice water, and let the sauce cool, stirring it occasionally. Serve at room temperature or slightly chilled.

Makes about 1/4 cup

Chocolate Lavender Cream Tarts

My husband says that I must have "unstitched the bag of my grandmother's sachet."
What does he know? I went outside and plucked a few stems of dried lavender last fall
and used them in my chocolate cream pie. (They are also available in some organic or
health food stores.) The combination is surprisingly and delightfully fragrant, and the
honey in the filling and cookielike pastry makes it even better. The pastry is quick and
easy-as-pie to make.

For the pastry

3 tablespoons unsalted butter, melted

1 tablespoon lavender or other honey

1 tablespoon sugar

Pinch of salt

¾ cup plus 2 tablespoons all-purpose flour

For the filling

¼ cup plus 3 tablespoons heavy (whipping) cream

1 teaspoon dried lavender blossoms

1½ ounces fine-quality bittersweet chocolate, chopped

½ ounce unsweetened chocolate

1 tablespoon lavender or other honey

1 large egg yolk

Pinch of salt

Confectioners' sugar

Prepare the pastry: Position a rack in the center of the oven and preheat the oven to 375°F.

Using a rubber spatula or fork, mix the melted butter, honey, sugar, and salt in a small bowl. Add the flour and stir until blended. Divide the dough into 2 halves; press each half into the bottom and up the sides of two 4½-inch fluted tart pans with removable bottoms. Prick the bottoms of the pastry shells with the tines of a fork. Place the tart pans on a baking sheet for easier handling and set aside. Bake until the pastry is dry and beginning to brown, about 8 minutes. Transfer to a wire rack and let them cool in the pans.

Reduce the oven temperature to 325°F.

Prepare the filling: Bring the cream and dried lavender blossoms to a boil in a small saucepan. Cover, reduce the heat, and simmer 5 minutes. Place the chopped chocolate in a small bowl; strain the hot cream mixture over the chocolate in the bowl, and stir until the chocolate is smooth. Stir in the honey, egg yolk, and salt until well blended. Pour the filling into the tart shells. Bake until the centers of the tarts are just set, about 15 minutes.

Transfer the tarts to a wire rack and let them cool completely. Sift the confectioners' sugar over the tarts before serving.

Makes 2 tarts

CHOCOLATE SHAVINGS

You will need to melt, then reform chocolate into a thicker bar to make it easier to shave.

Place 4 ounces of chopped chocolate in a microwave-safe bowl; microwave on medium power until it is soft, about 2 minutes.

Form a piece of heavy-duty aluminum foil into a rectangular $3 \times 2 \times 1\frac{1}{2}$-inch cup. Scrape the melted chocolate into the cup and let it cool until completely hardened.

Unwrap the block of chocolate and place it on a work surface covered with a piece of wax paper to catch the shavings. Scrape a melon-ball scoop or vegetable peeler lengthwise across the surface of the chocolate bar to make the shavings. You can store the chocolate shavings in a covered container in the refrigerator.

Chocolate Pineapple Custard Tarts

Tropical paradise describes this tart. Pineapple juice is reduced to intensify its flavor, then the syrup is baked into a creamy chocolate filling. It tastes refreshingly different. I have decorated each of these tarts with a tiny orchid, and they were lovely.

> 3 partially baked Basic Sweet Pastry shells (page 120), baked in 4 × 1⅜-inch or 4½ × ¾-inch tart pans with removable bottoms, still in the pans
>
> ½ cup pineapple juice
> ¼ cup heavy (whipping) cream
> 2 ounces semisweet chocolate, chopped
> 1 large egg
> 1 large egg yolk
> ½ teaspoon vanilla extract
> 3 tablespoons sugar
> 1 teaspoon cornstarch
> Pinch of salt
> ¼ cup diced fresh or canned pineapple

Position a rack in the center of the oven and preheat the oven to 325°F. Place the tart pans on a baking sheet for easier handling and set aside.

Pour the pineapple juice into a small, heavy saucepan; bring to a boil. Boil, uncovered, until the mixture has reduced to 3 tablespoons. Add the cream; cook over low heat until the mixture is hot, about 30 seconds. Remove from the heat; add the chocolate and stir until the chocolate is melted and smooth. Let the mixture cool.

Place the egg, egg yolk, vanilla, sugar, cornstarch, and salt in a small bowl. Whisk until it is smooth. Whisk in the cooled chocolate mixture until it is well blended. Pour into the tart shells, dividing it evenly.

Bake until the tarts are just set in the center, 28 to 30 minutes. Remove the baking sheet from the oven and transfer the tarts to a wire rack. Let them cool completely. Cover and refrigerate the tarts 1 hour or up to overnight. Remove from the refrigerator 1 hour before serving.

Just before serving, dust with confectioners' sugar and decorate with the diced pineapple.

Makes 3 tarts

Mocha Chocolate Pudding Tarts

If you order mochas at your local coffee shop, you will enjoy these tarts; the flavor of the filling reminds me of this chocolate coffee beverage. They are not too dark, not too sweet, but just right. The crust is easy to put together in a food processor; the tender cookie pastry that holds the filling is worth the effort to make your own.

For the crust

3 large egg yolks

2 teaspoons ice water, plus more as necessary

½ cup all-purpose flour

2 tablespoons sugar

1½ tablespoons unsweetened cocoa powder

Pinch of salt

¼ cup cold, unsalted butter, diced

For the filling

2 ounces bittersweet chocolate, chopped

1 ounce milk chocolate, chopped

1½ tablespoons sugar

½ cup heavy (whipping) cream

1 tablespoon strong brewed coffee

1 to 2 teaspoons unsweetened cocoa powder for finishing

Prepare the crusts: Lightly butter two 4½-inch-diameter tart pans with removable bottoms. Place on a rimmed baking sheet for easier handling. Set aside.

Whisk the egg yolks in a small bowl; measure out 1 tablespoon for the crust and place in a small bowl. Whisk the ice water into the bowl with the 1 tablespoon yolk, and chill while measuring the dry ingredients for the crust. Reserve the remaining beaten egg yolk for the filling.

Place the flour, sugar, cocoa powder, and salt in a food processor fitted with the knife blade. Pulse to combine, about three times. Add the butter and chilled egg yolk–ice water mixture; pulse until the mixture is well blended and holds together. Gather the dough into a ball on a piece of wax paper; divide it in half and flatten into two disks. Wrap each disk in plastic wrap and refrigerate for 15 minutes.

Roll out each pastry disk on a well-floured surface into a 6-inch round. Fit each pastry round into a prepared tart pan, pressing it up and into sides. Tuck the overhang into the inside of the pan for extra reinforcement, gently pressing the pastry into the grooves of the pan sides. If the dough is too soft to roll out, press it into the bottoms and up the sides of the tart pans. Pierce the bottoms of the pastry shell all over with the tines of a fork. Place the lined tart pans on a baking sheet and freeze until firm, about 15 minutes.

Preheat the oven to 375°F. Bake the tart shells until they are dry and firm, about 12 minutes. Let them cool completely on a wire rack. Reduce the oven temperature to 325°F.

Prepare the filling: Combine the chocolates in a small, microwave-safe bowl; microwave at medium power until glossy, about 1½ minutes. Stir until smooth.

Whisk the reserved egg yolks and the sugar in a small saucepan. Whisk in the cream and coffee. Cook over medium-low heat, whisking constantly, until the sugar dissolves, about 5 minutes. Remove from heat, and whisk in the melted chocolates.

Pour the filling into the tart shells. Bake until just set, about 20 minutes. Let cool completely; remove from tart pans.

Place the unsweetened cocoa powder in a fine mesh sieve, and dust lightly over the tarts before serving.

Makes 2 tarts

Peanut Butter Fudge Tarts

This filling has the texture of chocolate pecan pie, but with peanut butter flavor. It is creamy, but light, and the crunchy sweet peanut top is a nice touch. I love the tarts served hot with a scoop of vanilla ice cream that melts into a creamy sweet sauce.

> 2 partially baked Basic Pastry shells (page 118), baked in 4 × 1⅜-inch tart
>   pans with removable bottoms, still in the pans, or two jumbo muffin cups
> 1 ounce unsweetened chocolate, chopped
> ⅓ cup sugar
> 2 tablespoons smooth peanut butter (not natural-style)
> 1½ tablespoons light corn syrup
> 1 large egg
> ½ teaspoon pure vanilla extract
> Pinch of salt
> ¼ cup chopped, store-bought, honey-roasted peanuts
> Vanilla ice cream or sweetened whipped cream for serving

Position a rack in the center of oven and preheat the oven to 350°F. Place the tart pans on baking sheet for easier handling and set aside.

Place the chocolate in small, microwave-safe bowl; microwave on medium power until the chocolate is glossy, about 1 minute. Stir until the mixture is smooth. Let it cool.

CHOCOLATE SHARDS

*t*hese *will look rough, uneven, and like you just broke up a sheet of chocolate into crazy bits. But they look great piled on top of tarts and cakes.*

Line a baking sheet with aluminum foil. Place 2 ounces chopped bittersweet or semisweet chocolate in a small microwave-safe bowl; microwave on medium power until soft, about 1½ minutes. Stir until the chocolate is smooth.

Pour onto the aluminum foil, and spread into a very thin rectangle using the back of a spoon. Refrigerate the chocolate until it is very firm, about 30 minutes. Gently roll up the aluminum foil, crumbling the chocolate. Pour onto a foil-lined plate, and refrigerate until you are ready to use them.

Place the sugar, peanut butter, corn syrup, egg, vanilla, and salt in a medium mixing bowl, and whisk to blend. Whisk in the cooled, melted chocolate until blended. Pour the filling into the pastry shells, dividing it evenly. Sprinkle with the chopped honey-roasted peanuts, dividing them evenly. Bake until the edges of the tarts are slightly puffed and the centers are soft but set, about 25 minutes.

Remove the baking sheet from oven and transfer the tarts to a wire rack. Let stand until the tarts are cool enough to handle. Remove the tarts from the pans. Serve with ice cream or whipped cream.

Makes 2 tarts

Strawberry Chocolate Tarts

I know these tarts are not exactly baked, but the crusts are, so that qualified them for this book. They are what I look forward to making when firm, sweet summer strawberries are bountiful. The chocolate layer on the bottom tastes like dark fudge, with a little tang from the sour cream.

  3 tablespoons heavy (whipping) cream
  1 teaspoon light corn syrup
  2 ounces bittersweet or semisweet chocolate, chopped
  2 tablespoons sour cream
  2 fully-baked Basic Sweet Pastry shells (page 120), baked in
      4½ × ¾-inch tart pans with removable bottoms
  2 tablespoons fine-quality strawberry jam or sieved strawberry preserves
  ½ pint fresh strawberries, hulled and halved

Place the cream and corn syrup in a microwave-safe bowl; microwave on high power until simmering, about 25 seconds. Stir in the chocolate until smooth; stir in the sour cream. Let cool to lukewarm.

Pour the lukewarm chocolate mixture into the tart shells, and spread evenly. Chill until firm, about 30 minutes.

Heat the jam in a small microwave-safe bowl on medium power 10 seconds; stir until smooth. Brush or spoon onto the tops of the tarts to the edges of the pastry shells. Arrange the strawberries attractively on the tarts, cut sides down. Refrigerate until chilled, about 1 hour.

Remove the tarts from the pans and place on serving plates.

Makes 2 tarts

Chocolate Rum Banana Cream Pies

Homemade chocolate pudding is layered with bananas in these pies, and then you have three options for finishing them. My favorite is to caramelize the bananas on the top with the small torch that I often use when I wear my other hat as a food stylist. Then I spread them with the creamy, fluffy Marshmallow Meringue and bake them until the tops are toasty.

> 2 fully baked Basic Pastry shells (page 118), baked in 4 × 1⅜-inch tart
>   pans with removable bottoms, still in the pans, or in two jumbo muffin
>   cups lined with nonstick aluminum foil
>
> ¼ cup sugar
> 2 teaspoons all-purpose flour
> Pinch of salt
> ¼ cup whole milk
> 1 large egg yolk
> 1 ounce bittersweet chocolate, finely
>   chopped
> ½ ounce unsweetened chocolate,
>   finely chopped
> 1 tablespoon unsalted butter
> 1 tablespoon heavy (whipping) cream
> 1 tablespoon dark rum
> 1 small banana

2 teaspoons sugar or Rum Whipped Cream or Marshmallow
   Meringue (recipes follow)

Position a rack in the center of the oven and preheat the oven to 350°F. Put the tart pans on a baking sheet for easier handling and set aside.

Place the sugar, flour, and salt in a small, heavy saucepan. Whisk to combine well. Whisk in the whole milk and egg yolk until well blended. Place the saucepan over medium-low heat and cook, whisking constantly, until the mixture is thickened and coats the back of a spoon, 12 to 13 minutes.

Remove the saucepan from the heat and add the chocolates, butter, and cream. Whisk until they melt and the mixture is smooth, returning the saucepan briefly to the heat, if necessary. Remove from heat, and whisk in the rum. Transfer the pudding mixture to a bowl; place a piece of plastic wrap directly on the surface of the pudding, and let it cool to room temperature. Refrigerate until the mixture is cold, 1 to 2 hours.

Spoon half of the pudding mixture into the pastry shells, dividing it evenly. Slice half of the banana thinly and arrange on the pudding mixture, dividing it evenly. Spoon the remaining half of the pudding mixture on the banana slices, dividing it evenly. Slice the remaining banana diagonally into thin oval slices; arrange the slices attractively on the tops of the tarts.

To serve, sprinkle the banana slices with sugar. Caramelize the sugar with a torch, or place the tarts under a preheated broiler and broil until the sugar is caramelized. Serve with whipped cream on the side.

Or you can spread rum-flavored whipped cream over the bananas: Beat ¼ cup heavy (whipping) cream, 1 tablespoon confectioners' sugar, and 2 teaspoons rum in a small mixing bowl until firm peaks form.

Or you can caramelize the bananas and bake the pies with Marshmallow Meringue on top. Preheat the oven to 400°F. Cover the pies with Marshmallow Meringue, sealing the meringue to the edges of the tart pans. Bake the pies just until the peaks and ridges of the meringue are lightly browned, 4 to 6 minutes. Let the tarts cool 10 minutes. Carefully remove the tarts from the pans or muffin cups (peel off the foil), and serve while the meringue is warm.

Makes 2 pies

Marshmallow Meringue
If you lightly mist the measuring cup with cooking spray before measuring the marshmallow crème, it will not stick to the cup but will slide right out. Lightly mist the spatula, too.

> ¼ cup Marshmallow Creme, such as Kraft Jet-Puffed
> 1 large egg white
> Pinch of salt
> 1 tablespoon plus 1 teaspoon sugar

Preheat the oven to 400°F. Use a rubber spatula to measure marshmallow creme in a dry ingredient measuring cup and scrape it all into a small bowl. Stir it well; the creme will be sticky.

Place the egg white and salt in a small, deep mixing bowl; beat on high speed using a handheld electric mixer until foamy. Add the sugar and beat until firm, glossy peaks form. Stir 2 tablespoons of the egg white into the bowl of marshmallow creme until it is incorporated. (The marshmallow creme is very sticky and will be difficult to blend at first, but it will become easier as the remaining whites are folded in.) Fold in the remaining egg white. Spread the meringue on the pies, mounding slightly in the center and swirling to create peaks.

Bake the pies just until the peaks and ridges of marshmallow meringue are lightly browned, 4 to 6 minutes.

Makes 2 pies

၁၀

Chocolate Decadence Cheesecakes

The ultimate chocolate cheesecake is this one; a chocolate version of the rich and creamy New York cheesecake. They are perfect all on their own, but they are divine drizzled with Rich Caramel Sauce (page 244) or finished with one of the Crowning Glory for Cheesecakes ideas (page 105).

    Unsalted butter for greasing the cans

    5 chocolate cream-filled cookies, such as Oreo

    2 teaspoons unsalted butter, at room temperature

    2 ounces fine-quality semisweet chocolate, chopped

    4 ounces cream cheese, at room temperature

    ¼ cup sugar

    1 large egg

    2 tablespoons heavy (whipping) cream

    1 teaspoon pure vanilla extract

Position a rack in the center of the oven and preheat the oven to 325°F. Lightly butter the insides of two 8-ounce cans (see page 8). Place the cans on a piece of parchment paper and trace around the circumference. Cut out two parchment rounds and line the bottoms of the cans with them. Cut out two 11 × 2-inch strips of parchment paper, and use them to line the inside of each can; the parchment should reach the top of the cans. Place the cans in an 8- to 9-inch square baking pan and set the pan aside.

after the cheesecakes have baked and been refrigerated 6 hours or overnight, add these finishes, then refrigerate to set them before unmolding:

Shimmering Apricot Glaze: Heat $1/2$ to $2/3$ cup apricot jam in a saucepan over low heat until it melts; pour through a fine-mesh sieve over the cooled cheesecake and refrigerate until it sets.

White and Chocolate Swirled Ganache Topping: Place 2 tablespoons heavy cream in a small microwave-safe bowl; microwave at high power until hot, about 20 seconds. Stir in 2 ounces bittersweet chocolate, chopped, until it melts and the mixture is smooth. Let it cool to room temperature.

Place 2 tablespoons heavy cream in a small microwave-safe bowl; microwave at high power until hot, about 20 seconds. Stir in 2 ounces white chocolate, chopped, until the mixture is smooth. Let it cool to room temperature.

Pour the bittersweet chocolate ganache over the cheesecakes, tilting the pans so that the ganache will spread out to the edges. Using a teaspoon, drop dollops of the white chocolate ganache onto the glazed cheesecake tops, then use a wooden skewer or toothpick to stretch out tendrils of white chocolate ganache and swirl them across the surfaces of the cheesecakes.

Jewel Boxes: Prepare the bittersweet ganache and the white chocolate ganache as above. Let them cool to room temperature. Remove the cheesecakes from the cans and place them on a work surface. Pour the bittersweet ganache on the tops of the cheesecakes, dividing evenly; spread all over the tops and sides. Refrigerate 30 minutes or until the chocolate layer has set.

Meanwhile, place the white chocolate ganache in a pastry bag fitted with a small round tip, a squeeze bottle, or a small, heavy-duty zip-top bag; refrigerate until thick enough to pipe and firm enough to hold its shape after piping, about 1 hour. For the zip-top bag, snip a tiny corner of it to pipe; pipe the white chocolate ganache in lacy large-to-small swirls and intersecting arcs all over the bittersweet ganache-covered cheesecakes. Refrigerate until the white chocolate hardens, about 15 minutes. Fill in the circles with alternating colors of jewel box–colored cake decorating gel.

Candy Cane Cheesecakes: Prepare either the bittersweet ganache or the white chocolate ganache as directed above. Break about 20 soft peppermint sticks in half, and stand them up around the sides of the cheesecakes after the ganache is chilled and set.

Break up the cookies and put them in a food processor bowl fitted with the knife blade. Process until they are finely crushed, about 10 seconds. Add the butter and pulse until blended, about six pulses. Spoon the crumb mixture into the prepared cans, dividing it evenly. Gently press the crumb mixture down with your fingertips. Bake until the color of the crust begins to darken, 8 to 10 minutes.

Remove the baking sheet from the oven and transfer it with the cans onto a wire rack. Let the crusts cool. Keep the oven on.

Place the chocolate in a small, microwave-safe bowl; microwave on medium power until soft, 1 to 1¾ minutes. Stir until it is smooth. Let it cool.

Place the cream cheese and sugar in a small, deep mixing bowl, and beat with a handheld electric mixer on medium speed just until the mixture is smooth and creamy, about 30 minutes. Scrape down the sides of the bowl. Add the egg; reduce the mixer speed to low, and beat just until it is blended into the cream cheese mixture. Beat in the cream and vanilla. Beat in the cooled melted chocolate until blended.

Pour the batter into the prepared cans, dividing it evenly. Pour boiling water into the baking pan to come halfway up the sides of the cans. Bake until the cheesecakes are just set, 28 to 30 minutes. Remove the baking pan from the oven; transfer the cans to a wire rack, and let cool completely. Cover and refrigerate the cheesecakes 6 hours or overnight.

To serve, run a sharp knife around the sides of the cans to loosen the cheesecakes. Turn the cakes out, remove the parchment paper, and place them upright on serving plates. Garnish as desired. The cheesecakes will keep, covered, in the refrigerator for 1 week.

Makes 2 cheesecakes

Chocolate Coconut Macaroon Cheesecakes

This is a heavenly version of an already luscious dessert.

Ingredients for 1 recipe Chocolate Decadence Cheesecake (page 104)
¼ cup sweetened flaked coconut, plus additional sweetened flaked coconut
   for garnish, optional
½ cup diced, dark chocolate-covered coconut candy bars,
   such as Mounds
Dark Chocolate Ganache Glaze (recipe follows)

Prepare the crust for Chocolate Decadence Cheesecake, omitting the sugar; add ¼ cup flaked coconut to the crushed cookies in the food processor when you add the butter. Bake as directed.

Prepare the filling for Chocolate Decadence Cheesecake, and fold in the chopped candy bars. Pour into the prepared cans and bake as directed. Let them cool; refrigerate and unmold the cheesecakes as directed.

Place the cheesecakes on a wire rack. Smooth the glaze over the tops and sides. Sprinkle with additional coconut, if desired. Let stand 30 minutes before serving, or cover and refrigerate and store up to 2 days before serving.

Makes 2 cheesecakes

Dark Chocolate Ganache Glaze

¼ cup heavy (whipping) cream

½ cup (2 ounces) bittersweet chocolate chips

Bring the cream to a boil in a small, heavy saucepan. Remove from the heat and add the chocolate chips; swirl to submerge them in the hot cream. Let stand 1 minute; stir until smooth. Let stand until it reaches a spreading consistency.

Makes ⅓ cup

❧

FLAWLESS CHEESECAKES

Cheesecakes crack for several reasons. My job in writing this book was to make sure the recipes are correctly developed to eliminate as many of those issues as possible. For instance, if there is too much batter for the size of the pan, or can in small-batch cases, or the oven temperature is too high, the cheesecakes will crack.

You can help on your end, too. Your cheesecakes will turn out with smooth tops if you pay heed to these baking tips:

- Do not overbeat the batter. You need to mix it well, particularly the first step of beating the cream cheese and sugar until it is smooth. Get all the lumps out now, before you add the eggs. As you add the eggs and after they are in, you should mix the batter gently so as not to beat in air bubbles. Eggs hold in air and will release the bubbles as the cheesecakes bake; since the air has to go up, it will crack the surfaces to release the bubbles.

- Small-batch cheesecakes are baked in water baths for good reason; better not skip this step. When you put the cans inside a pan of hot water to bake, it "coddles" the cheesecakes and allows them to heat gently and evenly. If they are not in this bath, they have a tendency to overbake at the edges before the centers have a chance to heat the eggs to proper temperature. This condition will form deep cracks in the cheesecakes as they cool.

- Watch cooking times. About an inch of the centers of the cheesecakes will still be a little wobbly when the cakes are done—eventually the surfaces will smooth out as they cool.

- Always remember to run a knife around the edge to loosen the cake before unmolding. If the top does crack, consider concealing imperfections with fresh fruit or a berry or chocolate sauce.

Mocha Java Cheesecake

How can an already decadent chocolate cheesecake be any better? Well, you can add some coffee sugar syrup to the batter, spread chocolate mousse over the top, and sprinkle it with toffee. This is a small batch of Chef Franklin Biggs's Chef's Addiction cheesecake, a favorite at his restaurant, Homewood Gourmet, in Birmingham, Alabama.

2 tablespoons water
2 tablespoons sugar
1½ tablespoons instant dark coffee or espresso powder
Ingredients for 1 recipe Chocolate Decadence Cheesecakes (page 104),
    omitting the cream
1¼ ounces fine-quality semisweet chocolate, chopped
¼ cup heavy (whipping) cream
¼ cup toffee bits or crushed Heath bar

Combine the water and sugar in a microwave-safe bowl; microwave on medium power for 2 minutes, or until sugar is dissolved. Stir in the instant coffee or espresso powder until dissolved. Let it cool to room temperature.

Prepare the Chocolate Decadence Cheesecakes as directed in the recipe, substituting the espresso-flavored sugar syrup mixture for the 2 tablespoons cream in that recipe. Refrigerate the cheesecakes for 6 hours or overnight.

Place the chopped chocolate in a microwave-safe bowl; microwave on medium power until soft, about 1½ minutes. Stir until smooth. Let stand until the chocolate is cool but not set.

Beat the cream in a small, deep mixing bowl with a handheld electric mixer until firm peaks form. Reduce the mixer speed to low and beat in the cooled, melted chocolate until it is blended. Spread the whipped cream over the cheese-cakes; sprinkle with the toffee bits. Refrigerate the cheesecakes at least 1 hour or until the mousse topping is firm.

Makes 2 cheesecakes

Fudge Ripple Cheesecakes

There is a thick ribbon of fudge running through each cheesecake, so every bite is very chocolate and very vanilla. That way, you get the best of both worlds in a cheesecake.

For the crust

½ cup crushed chocolate wafer cookies, such as Nabisco

2 tablespoons sugar

2 tablespoons unsalted butter, melted

For the fudge ripple layer

2 ounces (⅓ cup) semisweet chocolate chips

3 tablespoons heavy (whipping) cream

1 tablespoon light corn syrup

For the filling

6 ounces cream cheese, softened

⅓ cup sugar

Pinch of salt

2 tablespoons sour cream

1 teaspoon pure vanilla extract

1 large egg

2 large egg yolks

Position a rack in the center of the oven and preheat the oven to 325°F. Lightly butter the insides of two 8-ounce cans (see page 8).

Place the cans on a piece of parchment paper and trace around the circumference. Cut out two parchment rounds and line the bottoms of the cans with them. Cut out two 11 × 2-inch strips of parchment paper, and use them to line the inside of each can; the parchment paper should reach the top of the cans. Place the cans in an 8- to 9-inch square baking pan and set the pan aside.

Prepare the crust: Place the crushed cookies and sugar in a small bowl. Stir in the melted butter until crumbs are evenly moistened. Spoon the crumb mixture into the prepared cans, dividing it evenly. Gently press the crumb mixture down with your fingertips. Bake until the color of the crust begins to darken, 8 to 10 minutes.

Remove the baking sheet from the oven and transfer it with the cans to a wire rack. Let the crusts cool. Keep the oven on.

Prepare the fudge ripple layer: Place the semisweet chocolate chips in a medium, microwave-safe bowl and microwave on medium power until soft, about 1½ minutes; stir until smooth. Stir in the cream and corn syrup.

Prepare the filling: Place the cream cheese, sugar, and salt in a medium mixing bowl and beat with a handheld electric mixer on medium speed just until the mixture is smooth and creamy, about 30 seconds. Add the sour cream and vanilla; reduce the mixer speed to low, and beat just until it is blended into the cream cheese mixture. Beat in the egg and egg yolks just until they are blended in.

Pour about half of the batter into the prepared cans, dividing it evenly. Drizzle about two-thirds of the fudge ripple layer over the filling. Spoon the remaining batter over the fudge ripple layer, and drizzle the remaining fudge ripple over the tops. Use the tip of a small sharp knife to swirl the fudge ripple into the top layer of the batter.

CHEESECAKES IN CANS VS. PANS

There are more than several makers of 4½-inch diameter cheesecake pans that are manufactured for baking miniature cheesecakes. There are many online sources and cookware shops where you can purchase them. The recipes in this book can be baked in them, but I prefer the size and shapes of the cheesecakes when they are baked in parchment-lined, 8-ounce cans such as water chestnut or bamboo shoot cans.

If you choose the miniature cheesecake pans, you will end up with wider cheesecakes that are not as tall and creamy. The cans are about 3 inches in diameter and will yield cheesecakes that are at least 2 inches tall—to me, a much better portion size for single servings.

Pour boiling water into the baking pan to come halfway up the sides of the cans. Bake until the cheesecakes are just set, about 30 minutes. Remove the baking pan from the oven; transfer the cans to a wire rack, and let cool completely. Cover and refrigerate the cheesecakes 6 hours or overnight.

To serve, run a sharp knife around the sides of the cans to loosen the cheesecakes. Turn the cakes out, remove the parchment paper, and place them upright on serving plates. Garnish as desired (see page 105 for cheesecake finishes). The cheesecakes will keep, covered, in the refrigerator for 1 week.

Makes 2 cheesecakes

ᕙᕗ

Turtle Cheesecakes

These are amazing. The crust is a layer of homemade brownie pieces fitted into the bottoms of the cans. Then a luscious layer of cream cheese mixture is swirled with creamy dulce de leche sauce, and they are topped with chopped Turtle candy.

Unsalted butter for greasing the cans
½ recipe Ultimate Brownies (page 169)
4 ounces cream cheese, softened
2 tablespoons sugar
¼ cup sweetened condensed milk
1 large egg
1 large egg yolk
1 tablespoon heavy (whipping) cream
2 teaspoons all-purpose flour
1 teaspoon pure vanilla extract
2 tablespoons dulce de leche or caramel sundae topping
½ cup coarsely chopped chocolate caramel candy, such as Turtles

Position a rack in the center of the oven and preheat the oven to 325°F. Lightly butter the insides of two 8-ounce cans (see page 8). Place the cans on a piece of parchment paper and trace around the circumference. Cut out two parchment paper rounds and line the bottoms of the cans with them. Cut out two 11 × 2-inch strips of parchment, and use them to line the inside of each can; the parchment paper should reach the top of the cans. Place the cans in an 8- to 9-inch square baking pan and set aside.

Cut the brownies into ½-inch pieces. Arrange the pieces in the bottoms of the prepared cans, pressing down lightly to form even crusts.

Place the cream cheese and sugar in a small, deep mixing bowl; beat on high speed using a handheld electric mixer until smooth and fluffy, about 30 seconds. Scrape down the side of the bowl. Beat in the sweetened condensed milk, egg, and egg yolk on low speed until smooth and blended, about 10 seconds. Scrape down the side of the bowl. Beat in cream, flour, and vanilla on low speed. Pour the batter into the prepared cans, dividing it evenly. Slowly drizzle 1 tablespoon dulce de leche sauce over the batter in each can in a thin, steady stream; the sauce will sink into the batter.

Pour boiling water into the baking pan to come halfway up the sides of the cans. Bake until the cheesecakes are just set, about 25 minutes. Remove from the oven; sprinkle the chopped candy over the cheesecakes, dividing it evenly. Return the cheesecakes to the oven and bake 1 minute more. Transfer the cans to a wire rack, and let cool completely. Cover and refrigerate the cheesecakes for 6 hours or overnight.

To serve, run a sharp knife around the sides of the cans to loosen the cheesecakes. Turn the cakes out, remove the parchment paper, and place them upright on serving plates. The cheesecakes will keep, covered, in the refrigerator for 1 week.

Makes 2 cheesecakes

෧෨

Basic Pastry

½ cup all-purpose flour
¼ teaspoon salt
¼ teaspoon sugar
3 tablespoons cold, unsalted butter, cut into small pieces and frozen
4 to 5 teaspoons ice water
Softened butter for preparing the pans

Combine the flour, salt, and sugar in a food processor; pulse to blend the ingredients. Uncover and sprinkle the butter pieces evenly over the flour mixture. Cover and pulse, using on/off turns, about 15 times, or until the lumps of butter reduce to the size of small peas. Uncover and sprinkle 4 teaspoons of ice water over the flour mixture. Cover and process just until small, moist clumps of dough begin to form, 6 to 10 seconds; add up to 2 teaspoons more ice water by teaspoonfuls if the dough is dry.

Tear off two sheets of wax paper and gather the dough onto one of the sheets. Form the dough into a mass, and divide it evenly in half. Form each half into a disk and wrap each individually in the wax paper. Refrigerate for 30 minutes.

Place a rack in the center of the oven and preheat the oven to 375°F. Lightly butter or mist with cooking spray two 4- or 4½-inch tart pans. Or line two jumbo muffin cups (1-cup capacity, 2½ × 1½-inch) with aluminum foil and lightly butter the foil. If using tart pans, place them on a baking sheet for easier handling, and set aside.

Roll out each pastry disk on a lightly floured surface into a 6-inch round. *If you are using tart pans,* fit each pastry circle into the prepared tart pan, pressing it into bottom edges and up along the sides. Tuck the overhang to the inside edge of the pan for extra reinforcement, gently pressing the pastry into grooves of the pan sides. *If you are using a muffin pan,* fit each pastry circle into a prepared muffin cup, pressing it into the bottom edges and up the sides, pleating the dough in even folds to fit it to the cup. Tuck the overhang to the inside for extra reinforcement.

Pierce the bottom of the pastry shells all over with the tines of a fork. Place the pastry shells on a baking sheet and freeze until firm, 15 minutes.

Line the pastry shells with aluminum foil, pressing it into the bottom and edges, and fill with pie weights, rice, or dried beans. Place the tart pans or muffin pan in the oven and bake for 15 minutes. Remove the pans from the oven and carefully remove the foil and pie weights. Return the baking sheet or muffin pan to the oven.

For partially baked crusts, bake until the crusts are just dry and set, about 5 minutes.

For fully baked crusts, bake until the crusts are light golden brown, about 10 minutes.

Makes 2 crusts

Basic Sweet Pastry

1 large egg yolk
½ cup all-purpose flour
2 teaspoons sugar
Pinch of salt
3 tablespoons cold, unsalted butter, cut into small pieces and frozen
2 teaspoons ice water

Softened butter or cooking spray for preparing the tart pans

Place the egg yolk in a small cup and beat it lightly with a fork. Measure out 2 teaspoons. Set aside the 2 teaspoons of yolk for the pastry, and save the rest for another use.

Place the flour, sugar, and salt in a food processor; pulse to blend the ingredients. Sprinkle the butter pieces evenly over the flour mixture. Cover and pulse, using on/off turns, until the lumps of butter reduce to the size of small peas, about 15 pulses. Sprinkle the water and 2 teaspoons beaten egg yolk over the flour mixture. Cover and process just until small, moist clumps of dough begin to form, 6 to 10 seconds; add up to 2 teaspoons more ice water by teaspoonfuls if the dough is dry.

Tear off two sheets of wax paper and gather the dough onto one of the sheets. Form the dough into a mass, and divide the dough evenly in half. Form each half into a disk and wrap them individually in the pieces of wax paper. Refrigerate 30 minutes.

Place a rack in the center of the oven and preheat the oven to 375°F. Lightly butter or mist with cooking spray two 4- or 4½-inch tart pans with removable bottoms. Or line two jumbo muffin cups (1-cup capacity, 2½ × 1½-inch) with aluminum foil and butter the foil. Place the tart pans on a baking sheet for easier handling and set the pans aside.

Roll out each disk of pastry on a lightly floured surface into a 6-inch round. *If you are using tart pans,* fit each pastry circle into a prepared tart pan, pressing it into the bottom edges and up along the sides. Tuck the overhang to the inside of the pan for extra reinforcement, gently pressing the pastry into the grooves of the pan sides. *If you are using a muffin pan,* fit the pastry rounds into the prepared muffin cups, pressing it into the bottom edges and along the sides, pleating the dough in even folds to fit it to the cup. Tuck the overhang to the inside of the pan for extra reinforcement.

Pierce the bottom of the pastry shell all over with the tines of a fork. Place the pastry shells on a baking sheet and freeze until firm, 15 minutes.

Line the pastry shells with aluminum foil, pressing it into the bottoms and edges, and fill with pie weights, rice, or dried beans. Place the tart pans or muffin pan in the oven and bake for 15 minutes. Remove the pans from the oven and carefully remove the foil and pie weights. Return the baking sheet or muffin pan to the oven.

For partially baked crusts, bake until the crusts are just dry and set, about 5 minutes.

For fully baked crusts, bake until they are light golden brown, about 10 minutes.

Makes 2 crusts

Rich Sweet Pastry

This is an excellent tart pastry; it is sweet, flaky, and stays crisp under a filling.

>   1 egg yolk
>   ¼ cup confectioners' sugar
>   ½ cup plus 1 tablespoon all-purpose flour
>   Pinch of salt
>   2 tablespoons plus 1 teaspoon unsalted butter, softened
>   1 teaspoon ice water, plus additional if needed
>   Softened butter or cooking spray for preparing
>   the tart pans
>   Additional flour for rolling out the dough

Place the egg yolk in a small cup, and beat it lightly with a fork. Measure out 2 teaspoons. Set aside the 2 teaspoons yolk for the pastry and save the rest for another use.

Sift the confectioners' sugar, flour, and salt into a food processor bowl. Add the butter, 2 teaspoons egg yolk, and water to the bowl; cover and pulse, using on/off turns, until the dough just begins to clump together adding additional ice water if the dough is dry.

Turn the dough out on a piece of plastic wrap and divide it in half. Shape each half of the dough into a disk and wrap it in plastic wrap. Refrigerate at least 1 hour and up to 24 hours.

Position a rack in the center of the oven and preheat the oven to 325°F. Lightly butter or mist with cooking spray two 4 or 4½-inch tart pans. Or line two jumbo muffin cups (1-cup capacity, 2½ × 1½-inch) with aluminum foil and butter or mist the foil. Place the tart pans on a baking sheet for easier handling and set aside.

Roll out each disk of pastry on a lightly floured surface into a 6-inch round. *If you are using tart pans,* fit each pastry circle into a prepared tart pan, pressing it into the bottom edges and up and along the sides. Tuck the overhang to the inside of the pan for extra reinforcement, gently pressing the pastry into the grooves of the pan sides. *If you are using a muffin pan,* fit the pastry rounds into the prepared cups, pressing it into the bottom edges and up and along the sides, pleating the dough in even folds to fit it to the cup. Tuck the overhang to the inside of the pan for extra reinforcement.

Pierce the bottom of the pastry all over with the tines of a fork. Place the pastry shells on a baking sheet and freeze until firm, 15 minutes.

Line the pastry shells with aluminum foil, pressing it into the corners and edges, and fill with pie weights, rice, or dried beans. Place the tart pans or muffin pan in the oven and bake for 15 minutes. Remove the pans from the oven and carefully remove the foil and pie weights. Return the baking sheet or muffin pan to the oven.

For partially baked crusts, bake until the crusts are just dry and set, about 5 minutes.

For fully baked crusts, bake until they are light golden brown, about 10 minutes.

Makes 2 crusts

ᕬ

COOKIE BLISS
Irresistible Treats

❦

These small-batch recipes allow you to fit in the time to bake cookies, batch after batch. You can make a different chocolate cookie treat every day because it takes much less time to make and bake the dough for just six to eight cookies.

Cookie baking should be a cherished ritual with your children, and now it is a more achievable process. I do not hesitate to go into the kitchen and pull out the flour and sugar canisters if my nine-year-old daughter gets a whim to make chocolate chip cookies (her favorites). With our combined efforts, we are eating cookies, warm and gooey with melted chocolate, in 20 minutes. That is less time than it would take for me to drive to the store for a package of cookies. And it is a whole lot more fun to bake with your little ones than rely on a store-bought cookie to make them happy.

There are drop cookies in this chapter that you may gobble up as soon as they come out of the oven, bar cookies that are close to one-bowl cookies, rolled cookies, cream-filled cookies, shortbread, biscotti, and cookies with oats, nuts, and coconut. You will make chewy cookies and crisp cookies; and you can find down-to-earth, old-fashioned favorites along with fancy cookies with updated flavors. And the best part? They are all richly full of chocolate.

The techniques for making small batches of cookies are the same as for preparing dozens, except that you need less equipment. (Cleanup is easier, too.) A handheld mixer is used for mixing the dough, and just one baking sheet will do the job.

You can even use your toaster oven and save the energy of heating up the oven. One of the questions people ask me is "why should I heat the oven for only a few cookies?" Well, you do not have to! As long as your toaster oven is well insulated and cooks evenly, you can trust it to bake your cookies.

SMALL-BATCH COOKIE BAKING BASICS

If you have made the effort to prepare the dough, you do not want to stop there at finessing the cookies. In other words, there are some bakers' secrets to making sure they bake evenly, with just the right browning so you do not have to cross your fingers that your oven finishes your work the way you hope.

1. Measure everything correctly. When you reduce ingredient amounts to make small batches, every spec of flour counts. See page 9 for measuring guides.

2. Use a heavy-duty aluminum baking sheet with 1-inch rimmed sides. You run the risk of burning the cookie bottoms if you use a thin, flimsy baking sheet. The baking sheets can be found at supermarkets and cookware stores. They are called half- or quarter-sheet pans at restaurant supply stores.

   I have a quarter-sheet pan that I use for almost everything in this book, from baking cookies to using it to hold cakes and tarts for easier handling to and from the oven. Do not run out and purchase expensive cookie sheets; these smaller, rimmed baking sheets are less expensive and will turn out beautiful cookies.

3. Line the baking sheet with a piece of parchment paper or a nonstick baking mat; the cookies will never stick, and to transfer them to wire rack for cooling, all you do is slide the parchment paper, with the cookies, onto the rack. You will not have to wash the baking sheet, either.

4. Be sure to preheat the oven for about 15 minutes so you know it has reached the correct temperature. If the cookie dough is slowly warmed in an oven that has not reached temperature, or if you put the cookie dough on a warm baking sheet right after cooking the first batch, the dough will melt and spread too quickly.

5. Let the cookies cool completely before storing them in an airtight container; otherwise, trapped steam will make them soggy. Layer them between pieces of wax paper if you are stacking them in the airtight container.

Simply the Best Small-Batch Chocolate Chip Cookies

My eight-year-old wants to make these every other day. They are her absolute favorite, and she has tasted close to every recipe in this book. She likes them because every bite gives you more chocolate than cookie. I like them for the buttery ring of crispy cookie around the edges—then your teeth sink into a chewy, gooey center. Thin, wrinkly, and bumpy with chocolate chips, this recipe sums up our dreams of a chocolate chip cookie.

By the way, here is a great illustration of why you should measure flour by spooning the flour into the measuring cup, then leveling it off, instead of dunking the measuring cup into the flour canister. When you do the latter, more flour packs into the measuring cup. I was in a hurry one day and dipped the measuring cup into the flour canister, thinking I would save time. The cookies were harder, fatter, and not as soft and chewy, and it was not a bit quicker to put together the dough. My daughter could tell the difference by looking at them, and so could I. Go for the spooning method to get these right!

½ cup all-purpose flour

⅛ teaspoon baking soda

⅛ teaspoon salt

3 tablespoons unsalted butter, softened

3 tablespoons firmly packed light brown sugar

3 tablespoons granulated sugar

1 tablespoon well-beaten egg or egg substitute

½ teaspoon pure vanilla extract

½ cup semisweet chocolate chips

¼ cup chopped pecans, optional

Position a rack in the center of the oven and preheat the oven to 375°F. Line a baking sheet with parchment paper and set it aside.

Place the flour, baking soda, and salt in a small bowl; whisk to blend.

Place the butter and sugars in a small, deep mixing bowl; beat with a handheld electric mixer on low speed until blended, about 20 seconds. Add the egg and vanilla; reduce the speed to medium, and beat until blended, about 10 seconds. Stir in the flour mixture with a wooden spoon; then stir in the chocolate chips and nuts, if using.

Spoon eight equal-size mounds of dough onto the prepared baking sheet, spacing them 2½ to 3 inches apart. Bake until the cookies are golden brown, 12 to 13 minutes.

Remove the baking sheet from the oven, place it on a wire rack, and let it cool 5 minutes. Slide the parchment paper, with the cookies, onto the wire rack and let them cool completely. Use a metal spatula to lift the cookies from the paper.

Makes 8 cookies

Brownie Cookies

"You can never be too rich or too thin" must have been coined to describe this cookie. Crisp on the outsides and chewy in the centers, the cookies taste like fudgy brownies with cookie texture perfection. I make them for all sorts of occasions: they are especially great for dunking in my morning latte. And, although they are rich, they are not overly sweet, so they are just right for late afternoon snack attacks. They hold up especially well when stirred into ice cream for your own cookies-and-cream concoction, and they make super ice-cream sandwiches.

> 2 ounces semisweet chocolate, chopped
> 1½ tablespoons unsalted butter
> ¼ cup firmly packed light brown sugar
> 1 tablespoon well-beaten egg
> ½ teaspoon pure vanilla extract
> ¼ teaspoon baking soda
> Pinch of salt
> ¼ cup all-purpose flour

Position a rack in the center of the oven and preheat the oven to 350°F. Line a baking sheet with a piece of parchment paper and set it aside.

Place the chocolate and butter in a medium, microwave-safe bowl; microwave on medium power until soft, about 1½ minutes. Stir until smooth. Stir in the brown sugar; whisk in the egg, vanilla, baking soda, and salt until well blended.

Stir in the flour. Cover and refrigerate until the dough is firm, about 30 minutes.

Spoon the dough by tablespoonfuls onto the prepared baking sheet, spacing them about 2 inches apart. Bake until cookies have puffed then flattened, about 14 minutes. Transfer to wire racks to cool.

Makes 7 cookies

∾

Chocolate Almond Scone Cookies

With the dense, buttery texture of scones and the rich taste of almond, not to mention yummy chunks of chocolate, this is the golden child of my cookie world. Soon after these come out of the oven, I retreat to the front porch swing with several of them, hoarding the first few for myself. You will, too!

½ cup all-purpose flour
½ teaspoon baking powder
⅛ teaspoon salt
3 tablespoons sugar
2 tablespoons almond paste, such as Solo brand
2 tablespoons plus 2 teaspoons unsalted butter, softened
1 tablespoon well-beaten egg
1 tablespoon sour cream
⅓ cup semisweet chocolate chunks or chips

Position a rack in the center of the oven and preheat the oven to 350°F. Line a baking sheet with parchment paper and set it aside.

Place the flour, baking powder, and salt in a small bowl and whisk to blend.

Place the sugar and almond paste in a food processor; process until they are well blended. Add the butter and egg; process until the mixture is smooth, about 30 seconds. Scrape down the food processor bowl once.

Add the sour cream to the processor and pulse to blend. Add the flour mixture and pulse to blend. Add the chocolate chunks and pulse just to mix them in.

Spoon the dough by rounded tablespoonfuls onto the prepared baking sheet, spacing them 2 inches apart. Bake the cookies until they are pale golden brown, 14 to 16 minutes.

Makes 8 cookies

Decadent Truffle Cookies

My stepdaughter works at the French Broad Chocolate Lounge here in Asheville, North Carolina, known as "ChoLo" to us locals. They sell exceptional truffles to taste along with the chocolate or coffee beverage of your choice. (And that is not all!) The owners/chocolatiers make worldly truffles such as French lavender, mole negro, masala chai, and Indian kulfi, as well as single origin truffles from beans of Peru, Ecuador, Hawaii, Madagascar, and Costa Rica. After one particularly rapturous chocolate-tasting there, I was inspired to capture the pure dark chocolate flavor in a cookie. The soft centers of the cookies are a little like the structure of truffles.

1½ ounces unsweetened chocolate, chopped

5 ounces semisweet chocolate, divided, chopped

1½ tablespoons unsalted butter, divided, softened

¼ cup plus 1 tablespoon sugar

1 large egg plus 2 teaspoons well-beaten egg from another large egg

2 tablespoons all-purpose flour

¼ teaspoon baking powder

Pinch of salt

1 cup semisweet chocolate chips

⅓ cup very finely chopped pecans or walnuts

1½ tablespoons heavy (whipping) cream

Position a rack in the center of the oven and preheat the oven to 325°F. Line a baking sheet with parchment paper and set it aside.

Place the unsweetened chocolate and 4 ounces of the semisweet chocolate in a small, microwave-safe bowl; microwave on medium power until soft, about 2 minutes. Stir until smooth. Let cool to room temperature.

Place 1 tablespoon of the butter, the sugar, the large egg, and the 2 teaspoons well-beaten egg in a mixing bowl; beat at high speed using a handheld electric mixer until very smooth and the sugar is dissolved, about 1 minute. Stir together the flour, baking powder, and salt in a small bowl; beat into the creamed mixture on low speed. Beat in the melted, cooled chocolates; fold in the chocolate chips and the nuts. Refrigerate the dough until firm, about 15 minutes.

Using a ¼ cup measuring cup, scoop mounds of dough onto the prepared baking sheet, spacing them 3 to 4 inches apart. Bake until the cookies seem puffy and are dry to the touch, about 15 minutes.

Remove the baking sheet from the oven. Slide the parchment paper, with the cookies, onto a wire rack and let them cool completely. Use a metal spatula to lift the cookies from the paper.

Place the remaining ½ tablespoon butter and the cream in a small, microwave-safe bowl; microwave on high power until very hot, about 20 seconds. Stir in the remaining 1 ounce chopped semisweet chocolate, mixing until smooth. Dip the cookies into the melted chocolate mixture; let cool on a wire rack until set, about 1 hour.

Makes 6 cookies

Chili Chocolate Pecan Crackles

Chili and chocolate make a great pair; they go into mole sauces, my best chili recipe, and they are two of a kind in spicy truffles. These cookies are crispy from the toasty pecans on the outside, and you bite into a chewy layer with a bite of pepper that lingers. Have a glass of milk ready, although I do love them with a tall, cold glass of stout.

¼ cup plus 3 tablespoons all-purpose flour
1½ tablespoons unsweetened cocoa powder
⅛ teaspoon ground chipotle chili powder
¼ teaspoon baking soda
Pinch of salt
1 tablespoon dark corn syrup
1 tablespoon well-beaten egg white
½ teaspoon pure vanilla extract
3 tablespoons unsalted butter, softened
3 tablespoons sugar
½ cup very finely chopped pecans

Position a rack in the center of the oven and preheat the oven to 375°F. Line a baking sheet with parchment paper and set it aside.

Place the flour, cocoa, chili powder, baking soda, and salt in a bowl; whisk to blend well. Set aside.

In a small bowl, whisk together the corn syrup, egg white, and vanilla.

Place the butter and sugar in a small, deep mixing bowl. Beat at medium speed using a handheld electric mixer until smooth and fluffy, about 20 seconds. Add the corn syrup mixture, and beat until blended. Scrape down the sides of the bowl and add the flour mixture. Beat just until it is blended. Refrigerate the dough to firm it slightly, about 30 minutes.

Roll the dough by rounded tablespoonfuls into seven balls; roll the balls in pecans. Place the balls on prepared baking sheet, spacing them 2 inches apart. Bake until the cookies are puffed and cracked, about 12 minutes. Slide the parchment paper, with the cookies on it, onto a wire rack and let them cool completely. Use a metal spatula to lift the cookies from the paper.

Makes 7 cookies

Chocolate Caramel-Swirled Peanut Giants

I have always said, if you are going to eat a cookie, go all out! These will convince you of the same. The cookie is deeply chocolate, with a caramel swirl inside that melts into the cookie and makes it moist and chewy on the inside. But you bite through a crispy crust that partly comes from some of the caramel swirl that sneaks out as they bake and crystallizes on the edges. The added candy bars and peanuts send these over the top!

4 ounces bittersweet chocolate, chopped (about ¾ cup)
2 teaspoons unsalted butter
¼ cup plus 2 tablespoons all-purpose flour
¼ teaspoon baking powder
⅛ teaspoon salt
¼ cup plus 2 tablespoons sugar
2 tablespoons well-beaten egg
½ teaspoon pure vanilla extract
2 fun-size (15-gram) dark chocolate Snickers bars, chopped
¼ cup chopped cocktail peanuts
2 tablespoons dulce de leche sauce or caramel ice cream topping

Combine the chocolate and butter in a small, microwave-safe bowl; microwave on high power until soft, about 2 minutes. Stir until the mixture is smooth. Let it cool to lukewarm.

Place the flour, baking powder, and salt in a small bowl and whisk to blend well.

Place the sugar and egg in a small, deep mixing bowl and beat with a handheld electric mixer on high speed until the mixture is thick and pale, 2 to 3 minutes. Beat in the lukewarm chocolate mixture and the vanilla until blended. Reduce the mixer speed to low and beat in the flour mixture just until blended. Stir in the candy pieces and peanuts with a wooden spoon. Drizzle the dulce de leche sauce over the dough, and fold in to swirl it into the batter but do not incorporate it. Cover the bowl and refrigerate the batter until it is firm enough to work with, about 30 minutes.

Position a rack in the center of the oven and preheat the oven to 350°F. Line a baking sheet with parchment paper and set it aside.

Spoon ¼ cup scoops of the batter onto the prepared baking sheet, spacing them 3 inches apart. Using a spatula, press the cookies down to flatten them slightly. Bake the cookies just until the tops are dry and cracked but still soft to the touch, 18 to 20 minutes.

Remove the baking sheet from the oven and slide the parchment paper onto a wire rack. Let the cookies cool completely on the paper. When completely cool, use a metal spatula to lift them off the paper.

Makes 5 cookies

Chocolate Coconut Pecan Tassies

I have tasted versions of this cookie for years, beginning with my tenure in the *Southern Living* magazine test kitchens. They were popular bite-size cookie tarts, and readers of the magazine sent in their versions—most often a simple cream cheese pastry baked with a candylike coconut and pecan filling. It was as hard to stop at one then as it is now.

Adding melted chocolate to the pastry and drizzling the tassies with melted ribbons of chocolate just makes them that much better.

> 1 ounce semisweet chocolate, divided
> 2 ounces cream cheese, divided, softened
> 1½ tablespoons unsalted butter, softened
> 1 tablespoon plus 1 teaspoon sugar, divided
> ¼ cup plus 1 tablespoon all-purpose flour
> 1 teaspoon well-beaten egg white
> ½ teaspoon pure vanilla extract
> 3 tablespoons sweetened flaked coconut
> 2 tablespoons chopped pecans, toasted

Position a rack in the center of the oven and preheat the oven to 325°F.

Chop ½ ounce of the chocolate and place it in a small, microwave-safe bowl; microwave on medium power until soft, about 1 minute. Let it cool; the chocolate should be cool but still soft.

Place the melted and cooled chocolate in a small, deep mixing bowl; add 1 ounce of the cream cheese, the butter, and 1 teaspoon of the sugar. Beat until smooth. Add the flour; beat until combined.

Roll the dough into six balls and place in ungreased miniature 1¾-inch muffin cups; press the dough into the bottoms and up the sides of the muffin cups. Set aside. Clean the mixing bowl.

Add the remaining 1 ounce cream cheese, the remaining 1 tablespoon sugar, beaten egg white, and vanilla to the mixing bowl; stir until smooth. Stir in the coconut and pecans. Spoon the mixture into the pastry cups.

Bake the tassies until the filling begins to brown on top, about 20 minutes. Remove from the oven and transfer the pan to a wire rack; let cool completely.

Meanwhile, finely chop remaining ½ ounce chocolate, and place in a small microwave-safe bowl. Microwave on medium power until soft, about 1¼ minutes. Drizzle the melted chocolate onto the cookies. Run a thin, sharp knife around edges of the tassies and remove them from the muffin cups.

Makes 6 tassies

Chocolate Oatmeal Cookies
with Macadamia Nuts

These little gems are chewy, cakey, chocolate drop cookies loaded with coconut. They are really pretty dotted with white chocolate and macadamia nuts.

½ stick (¼ cup) unsalted butter, softened

3 tablespoons firmly packed light brown sugar

3 tablespoons granulated sugar

1 tablespoon well-beaten egg

1 teaspoon milk or water

½ teaspoon pure vanilla extract

⅓ cup all-purpose flour

1½ tablespoons unsweetened cocoa powder

¼ teaspoon baking soda

Pinch of salt

½ cup old-fashioned rolled oats

3 to 4 tablespoons white chocolate chips

3 to 4 tablespoons chopped macadamia nuts

Position a rack in the center of the oven and preheat the oven to 350°F. Line a baking sheet with parchment paper and set it aside.

Place the butter and sugars in a small, deep mixing bowl; beat with a handheld electric mixer on medium speed until creamy, about 1 minute, scraping down the sides of the bowl once or twice. Add the beaten egg, milk, and vanilla; beat until blended.

Place the flour, cocoa, baking soda, and salt in a small bowl; whisk to blend. Add to the butter mixture and stir until blended. Stir in the oats, white chocolate chips, and nuts. Refrigerate the dough 30 minutes.

Drop spoonfuls of the dough onto the prepared baking sheet to make six equal-size mounds, spacing them 1½ to 2 inches apart. Bake the cookies until they are golden brown, about 15 minutes.

Slide the parchment paper onto a wire rack with the cookies, and let them cool completely. Use a metal spatula to lift the cookies from the paper.

Makes 6 cookies

◦∽◦

Chocolate Cherry Chunk Cookies

With unsweetened chocolate mixed with semisweet in the dough, and enough sugar to balance it, these drop cookies have a deep, dark chocolate flavor. Either semisweet or white chocolate chips are nice with the sweet-tart dried cherries.

¾ ounce unsweetened chocolate, finely chopped
½ ounce semisweet chocolate, finely chopped
1½ tablespoons unsalted butter
3 tablespoons all-purpose flour
⅛ teaspoon baking powder
Pinch of salt
1 tablespoon well-beaten egg
¼ cup plus 1 tablespoon sugar
½ teaspoon pure vanilla extract
¼ cup semisweet or white chocolate chips
¼ cup dried cherries

Place the chocolates and butter in a small, microwave-safe bowl; microwave at medium power until soft, about 1½ minutes. Stir until smooth.

Place the flour, baking powder, and salt in a small bowl. Stir with a whisk until blended.

Combine the egg and sugar in a small, deep mixing bowl. Beat with a hand-held electric mixer on low speed to blend. Increase the speed to medium and beat until lightened and pale in color, about 1 minute. Stir in the chocolate mixture and vanilla on low speed until smooth. Stir in the flour mixture on low speed until just combined. Stir in the chips and cherries. Cover and refrigerate the batter until firm, about 20 minutes.

Position a rack in the center of the oven and preheat the oven to 350°F. Line a baking sheet with parchment paper and set it aside. Drop the dough by heaping tablespoonfuls onto the prepared baking sheet, spacing them about 3 inches apart.

Bake until the tops of the cookies are cracked, 10 to 12 minutes. Slide the parchment paper, with the cookies, onto a wire rack and let them cool completely. Use a metal spatula to lift the cookies from the paper.

Makes 8 cookies

∾

Giant Triple Chocolate Oatmeal Chippers

My daughter woke up one Saturday determined to have a bake sale with homemade chocolate chip cookies. I had the ends of three packages of chocolate chips: semisweet, milk, and white, some oats I was planning on cooking for breakfast, and the standard cookie-making ingredients like eggs, sugar, and flour. So I was persuaded (pretty easily, actually) to skip the bowl of oatmeal and make cookies for us to eat and sell, with lemonade, later in the day. We had fun putting these together ("from scraps" instead of "scratch," as she calls it), and now we make them all the time.

⅛ cup all-purpose flour
¼ cup old-fashioned rolled oats
¼ cup firmly packed light brown sugar
¼ teaspoon baking soda
⅛ teaspoon salt
2 tablespoons unsalted butter, at room temperature
1 tablespoon plus 1 teaspoon well-beaten egg
½ teaspoon pure vanilla extract
Heaping ⅓ cup mixed semisweet, milk, and white chocolate chips

Position a rack in the center of the oven and preheat the oven to 350°F. Line a baking sheet with parchment paper and set it aside.

Place the flour, oats, brown sugar, baking soda, and salt in a medium mixing bowl and stir with a fork to blend. Add the butter and blend with the fork until moist crumbs form. Beat the egg and vanilla together, and add to the oat mixture. Blend it in with the fork or your fingers until a stiff dough forms. Mix in the chips with your hands.

Divide the dough into 3 portions and mound the portions on the prepared baking sheet, spacing them 4 inches apart. Bake the cookies until they are lightly browned, about 20 minutes.

Remove the baking sheet from the oven. Slide the parchment paper, with the cookies, onto a wire rack and let them cool completely. Use a metal spatula to lift the cookies from the paper.

Makes 3 cookies

∾

Oatmeal Chocolate Raisin Cookies

These are a version of the first cookie I ever learned to bake. My Aunt Cora's oatmeal cookies were chewy within but crisp on the outside edges—I think due to a bit more sugar. My daughter suggested adding chocolate-covered raisins instead of plain raisins, and they were a hit!

    ¼ cup (½ stick) unsalted butter, softened
    3 tablespoons firmly packed light brown sugar
    2 tablespoons granulated sugar
    1 tablespoon well-beaten egg or egg substitute
    1 teaspoon milk or water
    ½ teaspoon pure vanilla extract
    ¼ cup plus 2 tablespoons all-purpose flour
    ¼ teaspoon baking soda
    Pinch of salt
    ½ cup old-fashioned rolled oats
    ⅓ cup chocolate-covered raisins

Position a rack in the center of the oven and preheat the oven to 350°F. Line a baking sheet with parchment paper and set it aside.

Place the butter and sugars in a small, deep mixing bowl; beat with a handheld electric mixer on medium speed until creamy, about 1 minute. Scrape down the sides of the bowl once or twice. Add the beaten egg, milk, and vanilla; beat until blended.

Place the flour, baking soda, and salt in a small bowl; whisk to blend. Add to the butter mixture and stir until blended. Stir in the oats and chocolate-covered raisins.

Drop spoonfuls of the dough onto the prepared baking sheet to make six equal-size mounds, spacing them 1½ to 2 inches apart. Bake the cookies until golden brown, about 15 minutes.

Slide the parchment paper, with the cookies, onto a wire rack and let them cool completely. Use a metal spatula to lift the cookies from the paper.

Makes 6 cookies

∽

Triple Treat Macaroons

These cookies are light and airy from beaten egg whites, but they are more substantial than they appear. They are somewhat chewy and pack a lot of texture and flavor into each bite. I frankly think they are best enjoyed with a cup of espresso or a glass of port.

  ½ cup lightly packed sweetened flaked coconut
  3 tablespoons slivered or chopped blanched almonds
  1 large egg white, at room temperature
  ⅛ teaspoon cream of tartar
  Pinch of salt
  2 tablespoons sugar
  ¼ teaspoon pure vanilla extract
  3 tablespoons bittersweet or semisweet chocolate chips

Position a rack in the center of the oven and preheat the oven to 325°F. Line a baking sheet with parchment paper and set it aside.

Spread the coconut and almonds in a thin layer on a baking sheet and bake, stirring occasionally, until they are lightly browned, 12 to 15 minutes. Transfer the baking sheet to a wire rack and let the coconut and almonds cool completely. Keep the oven on.

Place the egg white and cream of tartar in a medium mixing bowl and beat with a handheld electric mixer on high speed until soft peaks form, about 20 seconds. With the mixer running, gradually add the sugar, 1 tablespoon at a time, and the vanilla. Beat until firm peaks form (not stiff and dry), 1 to 1½ minutes. Then gently fold in the cooled toasted coconut and almonds and the chocolate chips.

Spoon the macaroon mixture into eight equal-size mounds on the prepared baking sheet, spacing them 2 inches apart. Bake the macaroons until they appear dry, about 20 minutes.

Slide the parchment paper, with the cookies, onto a wire rack and let them cool completely. Use a metal spatula to lift the cookies from the paper.

Makes 8 cookies

Chocolate Caramel Thumbprints

"Let me do it!" has been my daughter's mantra since she was old enough to realize I was doing something besides changing her diaper. When we are in the kitchen together, I always have to find her cooking projects to help with. This is perhaps one of the first things I assigned her: to roll the cookies into balls and coat them in pecans. She still enjoys poking her fingers into the cookies to make the indentations. (They do taste sweeter when she does it.) All told, we love baking and eating these cookies in my house.

3 tablespoons all-purpose flour

2 tablespoons sugar

1 tablespoon unsweetened cocoa powder

Pinch of salt

1 tablespoon unsalted butter, softened

1 teaspoon beaten egg yolk

½ teaspoon pure vanilla extract

1 large egg white, lightly beaten

¼ cup very finely chopped pecans (almost ground)

3 vanilla caramels, unwrapped

1 teaspoon heavy (whipping) cream

3 tablespoons semisweet chocolate chips

Position a rack in the center of the oven and preheat the oven to 350°F. Line a baking sheet with parchment paper and set it aside.

Place the flour, sugar, cocoa powder, and salt in a medium bowl; mix with a fork to blend. Add the butter, egg yolk, and vanilla; mix well with the fork or your fingers until the dough holds together. The dough will be crumbly.

Shape the dough into five equal-size balls. Roll the balls in the beaten egg white, then in the pecans to coat. Place the balls 1 inch apart on the prepared baking sheet. Use your thumb to press an indentation in the center of each cookie. Shape the cookie sides with your fingers, if necessary.

Bake the cookies until the edges are firm, about 12 minutes. Meanwhile, place the caramels and cream in a small, microwave-safe bowl; microwave on medium power until the caramels soften, about 1½ minutes. Stir until smooth.

Carefully slide the parchment paper onto a wire rack. Spoon the caramel mixture into the cookie centers. Let the cookies and caramel mixture cool completely.

Place the chocolate chips in a small, microwave-safe bowl; microwave until soft, about 30 seconds. Use a fork to drizzle the melted chocolate over the tops of the cookies. Let stand until the chocolate sets.

Makes 5 cookies

Milk Chocolate Hazelnut Sandwich Cookies

Chocolate and hazelnuts are a perfect marriage, and I am not the first to note it. Candy makers know it, and so do the makers of Nutella, a chocolate-hazelnut spread that is always in my refrigerator. Peanut butter and Nutella sandwiches, with lots of granola sprinkled on the layers, is one I make often to pack in my dry bag for lunch when I go kayaking.

The silky milk chocolate and hazelnut-flavored spread is divine in this cookie filling, and it sets off the buttery hazelnut shortbread rounds perfectly. It is more of a grown-up cookie, and goes as well with a glass of bubbly as it does a cappuccino.

> ½ cup hazelnuts, toasted and skins rubbed off (page 156)
> ¼ cup all-purpose flour
> ¼ cup sugar
> ⅛ teaspoon baking soda
> Pinch of salt
> 2 tablespoons unsalted butter, softened
> 1 egg yolk
> Milk Chocolate Hazelnut Cream Filling (recipe follows)

Position a rack in the center of the oven and preheat the oven to 375°F. Line a baking sheet with parchment paper and set it aside.

Place the hazelnuts in a food processor fitted with the knife blade. Pulse until they are very finely chopped, about 25 times. Measure out ¼ cup of the chopped hazelnuts. Add the flour, sugar, baking soda, and salt to the remaining hazelnuts in the food processor. Pulse until combined, 2 or 3 times. Add the butter and egg yolk; pulse until well blended and the mixture holds together, 8 or 9 times.

Roll rounded teaspoonfuls of the dough in your hands to form twelve equal balls, and place them on the prepared baking sheet, spacing them 2 inches apart. Press the cookies to flatten them, using the bottom of a buttered drinking glass that is dipped in sugar; dip in sugar before flattening each cookie. Bake the cookies until they are beginning to brown at the edges, 11 or 12 minutes.

Transfer the cookies to a wire rack to cool completely. Sandwich two cookies together with Chocolate Hazelnut Cream Filling. Spread the reserved finely chopped hazelnuts on a plate and roll the edges of the cookies in the hazelnuts.

Makes 6 cookies

Chocolate Hazelnut Cream Filling
1 ounce fine-quality milk chocolate, chopped
1 tablespoon unsalted butter, softened
2 tablespoons confectioners' sugar
2 tablespoons Nutella

Place the chocolate in a small microwave-safe bowl; microwave at medium power until soft, about 1 minute. Stir until smooth. Let it cool to room temperature; the chocolate should be cool but still soft.

Mix the butter and confectioners' sugar into the cooled chocolate with a fork until smooth. Stir in the Nutella. Refrigerate until it reaches a spreading consistency.

Makes about ⅓ cup

TOASTING HAZELNUTS

hazelnut skins seem glued to the nuts, but toasting them loosens the skins and makes them easier to remove. And the nut flavor is more intense when they are toasted.

To toast the nuts, preheat the oven to 275°F. Spread the nuts in a single layer in an ungreased shallow baking pan, and bake until the skins crack and the nuts turn light golden brown, about 20 minutes. You can roast them at 350°F for a shorter amount of time, 10 to 12 minutes, but you must watch the nuts closely. They can darken and lose their mild sweet flavor in an instant. Wrap the hot nuts in a clean kitchen towel, and let them steam for 4 to 5 minutes; then rub vigorously to remove the skins.

Mini-Chocolate Sandwich Cookies

I am going out on a limb here, but I like these better than the chocolate cream-filled cookies that inspired them. The chocolate cookie part is more flavorful, buttery, and sweet; the filling is much like that store-bought cookie's, but it has a hint more butter flavor.

The small cookies make cute little ice cream sandwiches, too. My daughter loves them filled with a spoonful of strawberry ice cream instead of the vanilla cream filling.

> ¼ cup plus ½ tablespoon all-purpose flour
> 1½ tablespoons unsweetened cocoa powder
> ⅛ teaspoon baking soda
> Pinch of salt
> ¼ cup sugar
> 2 tablespoons unsalted butter, softened
> 1 large egg yolk
> 1 ounce fine-quality semisweet chocolate, melted and cooled
>   to room temperature
> Vanilla Cream Filling (recipe follows), optional

Position a rack in the center of the oven and preheat the oven to 375°F. Line a baking sheet with parchment paper and set it aside.

Place the flour, cocoa powder, baking soda, and salt in a small bowl, and whisk to blend.

Place the sugar, butter, and egg yolk in a small, deep mixing bowl; beat with a handheld electric mixer on low speed until blended, about 20 seconds. Increase the mixer speed to medium, and beat until the mixture is light and fluffy, about 20 seconds. Beat in the melted, cooled chocolate. Add the flour mixture to the egg mixture and beat just until the dough is blended, 15 to 20 seconds.

Portion and roll the dough in your hands to form twenty-four equal-size balls, and place them on the prepared baking sheet, spacing them 1½ inches apart. Press the cookies to flatten them using the bottom of a buttered and sugared drinking glass. Bake the cookies until they are firm, 8 to 10 minutes.

Transfer the cookies to a wire rack to cool completely. Sandwich two cookies together with Vanilla Cream Filling.

Makes 12 sandwich cookies

Vanilla Cream Filling
1 tablespoon unsalted butter, softened
1 tablespoon solid vegetable shortening or unsalted butter, softened
½ teaspoon heavy (whipping) cream, milk, or water
¼ teaspoon pure vanilla extract
Pinch of salt
½ cup confectioners' sugar, sifted

Place the butter, shortening, cream, vanilla, and salt in a small bowl and mix with a fork until a soft, smooth paste forms. Add the confectioners' sugar and mix until the filling is well blended and smooth. Cover and refrigerate the filling until firm enough to spread, about 15 minutes.

Note: To make larger sandwich cookies, form the dough into fourteen balls; press and bake 10 to 12 minutes, and fill the cookies as directed.

Makes about ¼ cup

Chocolate Chip Peanut Bars

Is this candy or cookie? It's hard to tell, but it is the best of both worlds: a fully loaded chocolate caramel peanut candy bar, like Snickers, on top of a buttery cookie layer, like Twix.

The dulce de leche sauce is very creamy and is worth the purchase price. It will last in your refrigerator for several months, so you can use a little at a time and it will not go to waste.

⅓ cup plus ½ tablespoon all-purpose flour, divided

2 tablespoons firmly packed light brown sugar

2 tablespoons unsalted butter, softened, plus butter for greasing the pan

1 teaspoon beaten egg yolk

3 tablespoons cocktail peanuts

¼ cup semisweet chocolate chips

2 tablespoons dulce de leche or caramel ice cream topping

Position a rack in the center of the oven and preheat the oven to 350°F. Line the bottom of a petite loaf pan (2-cup capacity, about 5 × 3 inches) with a strip of aluminum foil to fit down the length and up the short sides of pan, with enough extra length to extend over the edges by 1½ inches. Lightly butter the foil and set the pan aside.

Place ⅓ cup of the flour, the brown sugar, butter, and egg yolk in a bowl; mix together with a fork until it is well combined and crumbly. Press into the bottom of the prepared loaf pan. Bake until the crust is golden, about 10 minutes.

Sprinkle the peanuts and chocolate chips over the hot crust. Stir together the ice cream topping and the remaining ½ tablespoon flour; drizzle over the top. Bake until the caramel is bubbly around the edges, 12 to 13 minutes. Let it cool completely in the pan on a wire rack. Use the foil as handles to lift the cookie layer from the pan; carefully peel back the foil from the sides and cut into bars.

Makes 3 to 4 bars

Malted Milk Coconut Bars

The Easter bunny knew somehow to leave malted milk balls in my basket. Big as jaw breakers, I still pick them out of my children's stash. When I get a craving other times of the year, I make these cookies. That way I can wait for the bunny.

¼ cup plus 2 teaspoons all-purpose flour, divided

4 tablespoons firmly packed light brown sugar, divided

⅛ teaspoon baking powder

Salt

1½ tablespoons cold unsalted butter, cut into ½-inch cubes, plus butter
    for greasing the pan

1 tablespoon plus 1 teaspoon well-beaten egg, divided

⅓ cup sweetened flaked coconut

3 tablespoons chocolate malted milk powder

Pinch of baking powder (about ¹⁄₁₆ teaspoon)

Malted Milk Frosting (recipe follows)

Position a rack in the center of the oven and preheat the oven to 375°F. Line the bottom of a petite loaf pan (2-cup capacity, about 5 × 3 inches) with a strip of aluminum foil to fit down the length and up the short sides of the pan, with enough extra length to extend over the edges by 1½ inches. Lightly grease the foil and set the pan aside.

Place ¼ cup of the flour, 2 tablespoons of the brown sugar, the baking powder, and a pinch of salt in a medium mixing bowl; whisk to blend the dry ingredients. Add the butter cubes and the 1 teaspoon well-beaten egg; cut in the butter with a pastry blender until the mixture forms small clumps.

Press the dough evenly into the prepared pan. Bake until the crust is beginning to brown, about 10 minutes.

Meanwhile, place the remaining 2 teaspoons flour, the remaining 2 tablespoons brown sugar, the remaining 1 tablespoon beaten egg, the coconut, chocolate malted milk powder, baking powder, and a pinch of salt in a bowl; stir well. Pour the mixture over the partially baked crust. Bake until the filling layer is set, about 15 additional minutes. Let the cookie layer cool completely on a wire rack. Frost with hot Malted Milk Frosting; let stand until hardened, about 30 minutes. Use the foil as handles to lift the layer from the pan and cut into bars.

Makes 3 or 4 bars

Malted Milk Frosting
1 tablespoon unsalted butter
⅓ cup confectioners' sugar, sifted
2 tablespoons chocolate malted milk powder
2 teaspoons heavy (whipping) cream or milk
½ teaspoon pure vanilla extract

Place the butter in a small saucepan; cook over medium-low heat until golden. Stir in the sugar, malted milk powder, and cream; cook until the powder dissolves, 2 to 3 minutes, stirring constantly. Remove from the heat and stir in the vanilla; pour and spread the frosting immediately onto the cooled bar layer.

Makes about ¼ cup

Mississippi Mud Bars

Dark and goopy as the mud on the Mississippi River, these bars will soothe the most savage craving for chocolate. On top of the rich brownie layer, there is a layer of marshmallow creme and a thick layer of icing for your sweet tooth. Add chopped pecans to the brownies or the icing if you need the crunch.

> 3 tablespoons Marshmallow Creme, such as
>   Kraft Jet-Puffed
> 1 recipe Ultimate Brownies (page 169), just baked
>   and still hot
> Mississippi Mud Frosting (recipe follows)

Spread the marshmallow creme over the hot brownie layer. Cover and refrigerate until it's cold, 2 to 3 hours. Meanwhile, prepare the icing.

Spread the frosting on the chilled cookie layer; dip a knife in cold water to smooth out the frosting, if necessary. Chill until the icing is set, about 30 minutes. Cut into bars while cold; serve the bars at room temperature.

Makes 3 to 4 bars

Mississippi Mud Frosting
$\frac{2}{3}$ cup confectioners' sugar
2 tablespoons unsalted butter, at room temperature
$\frac{1}{2}$ teaspoon pure vanilla extract

2 tablespoons unsweetened cocoa powder, sifted

2 tablespoons evaporated milk or heavy (whipping) cream

Combine all the ingredients in a food processor; process until the frosting is smooth.

Makes about ½ cup

White Chocolate Raspberry Coconut Streusel Bars

If it were possible, I would have buttery streusel on all baked goods. I have been admonished for picking the streusel off of coffee cakes, muffins, and cookies if the underneath part did not hold up to the promise of the topping. These bar cookies do not have that problem. They are buttery good down to the last crumb. And they are super easy to put together; I have made them as a birthday gift for a co-worker, and it was a gift that she reminds me of often, as a hint!

Unsalted butter for greasing the pan
¼ cup sweetened flaked coconut
3 tablespoons sugar
⅛ teaspoon baking powder
Pinch of salt
½ cup all-purpose flour
2½ tablespoons unsalted butter, chilled, cut into ½-inch pieces
2½ tablespoons raspberry preserves
1¼ ounces fine-quality white chocolate, finely chopped, divided

Position a rack in the center of the oven and preheat the oven to 375°F. Line the inside of a petite loaf pan (2-cup capacity, about 5 × 3 inches) with aluminum foil. Lightly butter the foil and set the pan aside.

Place the flour, sugar, baking powder, and salt in a medium bowl and whisk to blend the dry ingredients. Add the coconut. Cut in the butter, using a pastry blender or your fingers, until the mixture is crumbly. Set aside ¼ packed cup of the flour mixture for the topping. Press the remaining flour mixture in the bottom of the prepared pan. Bake the crust until it appears dry and is beginning to brown, 8 to 10 minutes; it will not be fully baked.

Remove the pan from the oven, transfer it to a wire rack, and let it cool 15 minutes. Keep the oven on.

Spread the raspberry preserves evenly over the crust to within ¼ inch of the edges. Sprinkle three-fourths of the chopped white chocolate over the raspberry preserves. Sprinkle the reserved flour mixture over the white chocolate chips, patting gently to make an even layer. Bake until the top is light brown, about 20 minutes. Remove from the oven and let it cool completely on a wire rack.

Place the remaining white chocolate in a small microwave-safe bowl; microwave on medium power until soft, about 1 minute. Stir until smooth. Dip the tines of a fork into the bowl of melted white chocolate and drizzle over the bars. Let the cookie layer cool until the white chocolate is set, about 30 minutes. Use the foil as handles to lift the cookie layer from the pan and cut into bars.

Makes 3 to 4 bars

❧

Peanut Chocolate Chip Blondies

Blond brownies were my mother's comfort food, and I love them, too, although I have to add chocolate somehow. These butterscotch bars have all the compact moistness of a brownie, and they are particularly rich with chocolate chips and peanuts. Have a tall glass of milk handy . . .

½ cup all-purpose flour
¼ teaspoon baking powder
⅛ teaspoon salt
½ cup firmly packed light brown sugar
3 tablespoons well-beaten egg
1 tablespoon unsalted butter or margarine, melted
½ teaspoon pure vanilla extract
⅓ cup semisweet chocolate chips
⅓ cup cocktail peanuts

Position a rack in the center of the oven and preheat the oven to 350°F. Line the bottom of an 8 × 4-inch loaf pan with a strip of aluminum foil to fit down the length and up the short sides, with enough extra length to extend over the edges by about 1½ inches. Lightly butter the foil and set the pan aside.

Place the flour, baking powder, and salt in a medium mixing bowl and whisk to blend the dry ingredients.

Place the brown sugar, egg, butter, and vanilla in a small bowl and whisk to blend. Add the egg mixture to the flour mixture and whisk until blended. Stir in the chocolate chips and peanuts. Spoon the batter into the prepared pan, and bake until the top is golden and dry, 23 to 25 minutes.

Remove the loaf pan from the oven and transfer it to a wire rack. Let the cookie layer cool completely in the pan. Use the foil to lift the cookie layer from the pan; carefully peel back the foil from the sides and cut into bars.

Makes 4 bars

Ultimate Brownies

The first brownie recipe I made for *Small-Batch Baking* was really very good. After juggling ingredients to see if I could make it better, however, these are superlative. Moist, light, fudgy, and cakey all at the same time, they are delicious on their own or embellished with the many flavor additions on the next few pages.

> 1 ounce unsweetened chocolate
> 2 tablespoons unsalted butter
> ½ cup sugar
> 1 large egg, slightly beaten
> ½ teaspoon pure vanilla extract
> ⅛ teaspoon salt
> 3 tablespoons all-purpose flour
> ⅓ cup chopped pecans or walnuts, toasted, optional

Place a rack in the center of the oven and preheat the oven to 350°F. Line the bottom of a petite loaf pan (2-cup capacity, 5 × 3 inches) with a strip of aluminum foil to fit down the length and up the short sides of the pan, with enough extra length to extend over the edges by 1½ inches. Lightly butter the foil and set the pan aside.

Place the chocolate and butter in a microwave-safe bowl; microwave on medium power until the chocolate is soft and the butter is melted, about 1 to 1½ minutes. Stir until smooth. Stir in the sugar until blended. Stir in the egg, vanilla, and salt just until blended. Mix in the flour just until incorporated. Stir in the nuts, if using.

Spread the batter evenly in the prepared pan; bake until a toothpick inserted in the center comes out with a few moist crumbs attached, 27 to 28 minutes. Let cool on a wire rack for 10 minutes; use the foil as handles to lift the brownie layer from the pan and let cool completely on the rack. Cut into bars.

Makes 3 brownies

Variations

To make Dulce de Leche Brownies, prepare the batter and spread it into the pan. Drop 2 tablespoons store-bought dulce de leche, by teaspoonfuls, onto the brownie batter. Using the tip of a knife, swirl it gently into the batter. Chop a fun-size chocolate and caramel candy bar, such as Snickers or 100 Grand, and sprinkle it on the top of the batter. Bake, cool, and cut as directed.

To make Coconut Dream Brownies, prepare the batter; sprinkle one 1.9-ounce Mounds bar, cut into ½-inch pieces, over the batter, and press down gently into the top of the batter. Bake, cool, and cut as directed.

To make Top-Loaded Brownies, save the nuts for the top. Bake the brownies as directed; when they are done, sprinkle the nuts and ⅓ cup semisweet chocolate chips on top. Bake 1 minute to melt chocolate, then let cool as directed.

YUMMYLICIOUS ICE CREAM CAKES

from one small batch of Ultimate Brownies on page 169, you can make an unbelievably fabulous miniature ice cream cake.

Bake the brownie layer according to the recipe directions and let it cool completely; do not cut it. Remove the brownie layer from the pan and discard the aluminum foil that lined the pan; carefully slice the brownie layer in half horizontally using a sharp knife.

Line the pan again with plastic wrap or foil. Place the bottom brownie layer, cut side up, in the bottom of the lined pan. Spread the ice cream filling on top of the layer; then replace the top brownie layer, cut side down. Spread the Chocolate Ice Cream Cake Glaze (recipe follows) on top of the cake, and freeze the cake until it is very firm, 4 to 6 hours, before you remove it from the pan and cut it into slices.

Here are some of my very favorite ice-cream cake combinations:

- **Peppermint Chocolate Ice Cream Cake** Let 1 cup of vanilla ice cream soften slightly; stir in $1/4$ cup chopped red- and white-striped hard peppermint candies and $1/8$ to $1/4$ teaspoon peppermint extract, or to taste. Spread the peppermint ice cream between the brownie layers; spoon and spread the Chocolate Glaze (recipe follows) over the cake and freeze.

- **Chocolate Peanut Butter Ice Cream Cake** Let 1 cup of vanilla ice cream soften slightly; stir in $1/3$ cup chopped chocolate-covered peanuts and 3 tablespoons peanut butter. Spread the chocolate peanut butter ice cream between the brownie layers; spoon and spread the Chocolate Glaze (recipe follows) over the cake and freeze.

- **Coffee-Spiced Rum Chocolate Ice Cream Cake** Let 1 cup of coffee ice cream soften slightly; stir in 3 tablespoons chopped crystallized ginger and 1 tablespoon dark rum. Spread the ice cream mixture between the brownie layers; spoon and spread the Chocolate Glaze (recipe follows) over the cake and freeze.

- **Chocolate Caramel Ice Cream Cake** Spread 1 cup of dulce de leche ice cream on the bottom brownie layer; drizzle with 2 tablespoons dulce de leche or caramel ice cream topping. Replace the top brownie layer, cut side down, and spoon and spread the Chocolate Glaze (recipe follows) over the cake and freeze.

- **Chocolate Ice Cream Cake Glaze**
  2 tablespoons heavy (whipping) cream
  1 tablespoon light corn syrup
  1 1/2 ounces bittersweet or semisweet chocolate, chopped

  Place the cream and corn syrup in a small microwave-safe bowl; microwave at high power until very hot, about 30 seconds. Add the chocolate; stir until smooth. Let the glaze cool to room temperature before using.

  Makes 1/4 cup

S'Mores Brownies

What kind of Girl Scout would I be if I did not have some kind of s'mores recipe in here? I went all the way through the program and am still looking for good reasons to eat them! My daughter is a Daisy Scout now, so I am looking forward to years of campfires and toasty snacks. Meanwhile, I will bake these layers of graham cracker crusts, brownies, nuts, chocolate, and marshmallows to get my fix of s'mores.

⅓ cup graham cracker crumbs

1 tablespoon unsalted butter, melted

1 ounce unsweetened chocolate, chopped

2 tablespoons unsalted butter

½ cup sugar

1 tablespoon unsweetened cocoa powder

1 large egg, lightly beaten

½ teaspoon pure vanilla extract

⅛ teaspoon salt

3 tablespoons all-purpose flour

⅓ cup chopped pecans or walnuts, toasted, optional

¼ cup semisweet chocolate chips

½ cup mini marshmallows

Place a rack in the center of the oven and preheat the oven to 350°F. Line the bottom of a petite loaf pan (2-cup capacity, about 5 × 3 inches) with a strip of aluminum foil to fit down the length and up the short sides of the pan, with enough extra length to extend over the edges by 1½ inches. Lightly butter the foil and set the pan aside.

Mix the graham cracker crumbs and the melted butter in a small bowl until blended. Press the mixture into the bottom of the prepared loaf pan. Bake until it is light golden brown, 7 to 8 minutes.

Place the unsweetened chocolate and 2 tablespoons butter in a medium, microwave-safe bowl; microwave on medium power until chocolate is soft and butter is melted, about 1½ minutes. Stir until smooth. Add the sugar and cocoa powder and whisk the mixture to blend. Whisk in the egg, vanilla, and salt. Stir in the flour. Stir in the nuts, if using. Spread the mixture evenly over the crust in the pan.

Bake the brownies until a toothpick inserted in the center comes out with moist crumbs attached, 27 to 28 minutes; the top will appear puffed and slightly cracked. Do not overcook.

Remove from the oven and turn on the oven broiler. Scatter the chocolate chips over the brownies; cover with marshmallows. Broil until the marshmallows are lightly browned, about 1 minute. Let the brownie layer cool completely in pan on a wire rack.

Lift the cooled brownies from the pan using the foil as handles. Cut into bars.

Makes 3 to 4 brownies

Praline Brownie Cake

When I was growing up, my family took road trips for vacations. Wherever there was a Stuckey's along the way, we stopped for pralines. I learned to love them during those car rides, and have made semblances of the sugar, butter, nut candy discs ever since.

This praline topping reminds me of that childhood treat. It sits on a most decadent fudge-slathered brownie layer, which cuts more easily if the bars are cold.

For the ganache
1 ounce semisweet or bittersweet chocolate, chopped

1 tablespoon unsalted butter, cubed

2 tablespoons heavy (whipping) cream

1 recipe Ultimate Brownies (page 169), baked, omitting nuts, still in the pan

For the praline
¼ cup packed dark brown sugar

1 tablespoon heavy (whipping) cream

1 tablespoon unsalted butter

¼ cup confectioners' sugar

½ teaspoon pure vanilla extract

⅓ cup chopped pecans, toasted

Prepare the ganache: Place the chocolate and butter in a small microwave-safe bowl; microwave on medium power until soft, about 1½ minutes. Stir until smooth. Stir in the cream, and let the mixture cool until spreading consistency, about 15 minutes. Pour the ganache over the top of brownie layer, spreading to the edges. Chill 1 hour.

Prepare the praline: Place the dark brown sugar, cream, and butter in a small, heavy saucepan; bring to a boil, stirring until the sugar dissolves. Boil 30 seconds. Remove from the heat; whisk in the confectioners' sugar, vanilla, and pecans. Quickly pour the mixture over the top of the cake. Let the brownie layer stand until the praline cools and hardens, about 1 hour. Lift the cooled brownies from the pan using the foil as handles. Cut into bars.

Makes 3 to 4 bars

Espresso Brownies with White Chocolate Cappuccino Ganache

Most days, after our workout, my husband and I stop by our local Dripolater coffee shop here in Asheville. The baristas are so passionate about the farm-to-cup process that I have learned much from them about the nuances of flavors derived from growing regions of the world. Joining them for cupping, we taste new shipments of coffee and discuss the beans like you would wine.

Being the fan I am, I naturally add coffee to many baked desserts, and this is at the top of the list. The brownies are moist and chewy, with a decadent frosting.

1 ounce unsweetened chocolate
2 tablespoons unsalted butter, plus butter for greasing the pan
¼ cup plus 2 tablespoons sugar
1 large egg, plus 2 teaspoons beaten egg from another egg
½ teaspoon instant dark coffee or espresso powder
½ teaspoon pure vanilla extract
⅛ teaspoon salt
3 tablespoons all-purpose flour
⅓ cup chopped pecans or walnuts, toasted, optional
White Chocolate Cappuccino Ganache (recipe follows)

Position a rack in the center of the oven and preheat the oven to 350°F. Line the bottom of a petite loaf pan (2-cup capacity, about 5 × 3 inches) with a strip of aluminum foil to fit down the length and up the short sides of the pan, with enough extra length to extend over the edges by 1½ inches. Lightly butter the foil and set the pan aside.

Place the chocolate and butter in a medium, microwave-safe bowl; microwave on medium power until the chocolate is soft and the butter is melted, 1 to 1½ minutes. Stir until smooth. Stir in the sugar until blended. Stir in the egg, 2 teaspoons beaten egg, instant dark coffee or espresso powder, vanilla, and salt just until blended. Mix in the flour just until incorporated. Stir in the nuts, if using.

Spread the batter evenly in the prepared pan. Bake the brownie layer until a toothpick inserted in center comes out with a few moist crumbs attached, 26 to 28 minutes. Let cool on a wire rack 10 minutes; use the foil as handles to lift the brownie layer from the pan and let cool completely on a wire rack. Spread with the White Chocolate Cappuccino Ganache and let it stand until the ganache hardens, about 1 hour. Peel back the aluminum foil and cut into bars.

Makes 3 brownies

White Chocolate Cappuccino Ganache
2 tablespoons heavy (whipping) cream
2 tablespoons brewed dark coffee or espresso powder
Pinch of ground cinnamon
2 ounces fine-quality white chocolate, chopped

Place the cream, coffee, and cinnamon in a small, microwave-safe bowl; microwave on high power until simmering, about 30 seconds. Add the white chocolate; let it stand 1 minute for the white chocolate to soften, then stir the ganache until smooth. Let cool until it reaches a spreading consistency.

Makes about ⅓ cup

Chocolate Almond Candy Shortbread

I have to hide these bars when I make them if I want to eat any. The recipe for the almond shortbread is foolproof, and the thick layer of melted milk chocolate bar flavored with honey and flecked with almond nougat is simple to melt and pour over the cookie layer. After the chocolate firms up, the cookies cut well into bars or small triangles.

> ¼ cup slivered almonds, lightly toasted
> ¼ cup all-purpose flour
> ¼ cup confectioners' sugar
> ⅛ teaspoon salt
> 2 tablespoons cold, unsalted butter, diced
> Half a 3.52-ounce Toblerone chocolate bar (Swiss milk chocolate bar
>   with honey and almond nougat), coarsely chopped

Position a rack in the center of the oven and preheat the oven to 350°F. Line the bottom of a petite loaf pan (2-cup capacity, about 5 × 3 inches) with a strip of aluminum foil to fit down the length and up the short sides of the pan, with enough extra length to extend over the edges by 1½ inches. Lightly butter the foil and set the pan aside.

Place the almonds in a food processor fitted with the knife blade. Process until finely chopped, about 10 seconds; some pieces will appear ground. Add the flour, confectioners' sugar, and salt; pulse until well combined, about 3 times. Add the butter pieces and process until the mixture is crumbly, about 6 seconds. Transfer the crumb mixture to the prepared loaf pan and use your fingers to press it into an even layer.

Bake the shortbread layer until lightly golden, about 16 minutes. Sprinkle the chocolate pieces on the hot shortbread; return the pan to oven for 2 minutes more. Place the pan on a wire rack and smooth the melted chocolate on top of the shortbread layer using the back of a spoon. Let it cool completely; refrigerate to set the chocolate. Use the foil as handles to lift the cookies from the pan. Cut into bars or triangles.

Makes 3 or 4 bars

Dark Chocolate Pistachio Shortbread

The elite pistachio was not always so readily available in this country, certainly not without their shells. In 1969 there were only 600 acres of pistachio trees in California, the prominent growing area in this country. Now there are close to 50,000 acres of trees. Technology has driven increased production and more efficient distribution, so now we can eat and cook with them by the handfuls instead of shelling them ourselves until our fingers hurt.

That all works for me, because I love chocolate and pistachios together. The hint of sweet spicy cardamom makes this shortbread even more special.

> ¼ cup plus 1 tablespoon all-purpose flour
>
> ¼ cup roasted, unsalted shelled pistachios
>
> ¼ cup confectioners' sugar
>
> 1½ tablespoons unsweetened cocoa powder
>
> Pinch of ground cardamom
>
> Pinch of salt
>
> 2½ tablespoons unsalted butter, cut into pieces, softened
>
> ¼ cup confectioners' sugar mixed with 1 tablespoon unsweetened
>   cocoa powder

Position a rack in the center of the oven and preheat the oven to 375°F. Line the bottom of a 9 × 5-inch loaf pan with a strip of aluminum foil to fit down the length and up the short sides of the pan, with enough length to extend over the edges by 1½ inches. Lightly butter the foil and set the pan aside.

Place the flour, pistachios, confectioners' sugar, cocoa powder, cardamom, and salt in the bowl of a food processor fitted with the knife blade. Pulse the mixture until the pistachios are finely chopped, about 14 pulses. Add the butter pieces and pulse just until the mixture holds together.

Turn the dough out onto a piece of plastic wrap and knead it lightly to make sure the dough is just blended. Press the dough evenly into the prepared loaf pan. Using the tip of a sharp knife, score the dough into eight rectangles. Bake until the cookie layer is dry to the touch, about 15 minutes. Transfer the pan to a wire rack; recut the hot cookies into rectangles. Let the cookies cool completely in the pan. Use the foil to lift them from the pan. Dust with confectioners' sugar mixture just before serving.

Makes 8 cookies

Chocolate Rasberry Cake Hearts, page 44

Red Velvet Cake with White Chocolate Cream Cheese Frosting, page 23

Chocolate Derby Pecan Tarts, page 290

Chocolate Cherry Chunk Cookies, page 144

Cinnamon Chocolate Scones, page 240

Chocolate Coconut Macaroon Cheesecake page 108

Bittersweet Truffle Tarts with Salted Pistachio Brittle, page 283

Mississippi Mud Bars, page 163

White Chocolate Lemon Crème Brûlée, page 212

Salted Chocolate Caramel Tart, page 76

Cashew Toffee Crunch Chocolate Torte, page 50

Chocolate Rasberry Pots de Crème, page 214

Classic Chocolate Cake with Sour Cream Chocolate Ganache, page 17

Chocolate Baklava, page 251

Diva Milk Chocolate Layer Cake, page 20

Alisia's Chocolate Martini with Chocolate Sugar Cookies with Ganache Cookie Filling, page 321

Chocolate Toffee Biscotti

The chocolate-covered toffee bar that my father loved so well was initially made by hand by the Heath brothers in 1928. By World War II, they were distributing them to the military, which is where he first had them. When I baked with my dad, we often chopped or crushed Heath bars and put them in cookies, breads, and on top of cakes. It is a family tradition. This twice-baked dunking cookie is a perfect place for the crushed candy bar.

½ cup plus 1 tablespoon all-purpose flour
¼ teaspoon baking powder
⅛ teaspoon ground cinnamon
Pinch of salt
1 large egg yolk
3 tablespoons sugar
2 tablespoons unsalted butter, melted and cooled
½ teaspoon pure vanilla extract
⅓ cup plus ¼ cup miniature semisweet chocolate chips, divided
¼ cup finely chopped milk chocolate-covered toffee bar or toffee bits
½ teaspoon solid vegetable shortening
Additional finely chopped milk chocolate–covered toffee bar or toffee bits, optional

Position a rack in the center of the oven and preheat the oven to 350°F. Line a baking sheet with parchment paper and set it aside.

Place the flour, baking powder, cinnamon, and salt in a small, deep mixing bowl and whisk to blend.

Place the egg yolk, sugar, melted butter, and vanilla in a small bowl and whisk to blend. Add the egg mixture to the flour mixture and stir until a stiff dough forms. Knead in ⅓ cup of the chocolate chips and the chopped candy bar or toffee bits.

Lightly flour a work surface, and flour your hands. Transfer the dough to the work surface and form it into a 5 × 2 × 1-inch log. Place the log on the prepared baking sheet. Bake until it is golden brown and dry when lightly touched, about 20 minutes.

Remove the baking sheet from the oven and gently transfer the log with a metal spatula to a wire rack to cool completely. Leave the parchment paper on the baking sheet. Turn the oven off.

When the log is cool, preheat the oven to 325°F.

Cut the cooled log diagonally with a serrated knife into 10 slices. Arrange them, cut sides down, on the parchment paper–lined baking sheet and bake until they are dry and golden brown, 12 to 15 minutes.

Remove the baking sheet from the oven and, using a thin spatula, turn the biscotti over. Return the biscotti to the oven and continue baking until they are slightly dry, 12 to 15 minutes. Remove the baking sheet from the oven and slide the parchment paper onto a wire rack. Let biscotti cool completely.

Place the remaining ¼ cup chocolate chips and the shortening in a small microwave-safe bowl; microwave on medium power until soft, about 45 seconds. Stir until smooth. Dip one end of each biscotti into the melted chocolate mixture. Place on a piece of wax paper. If desired, sprinkle with the additional chopped candy bar, and refrigerate the biscotti until the milk chocolate hardens, about 20 minutes.

Makes 10 biscotti

Dark Sweet Chocolate
Almond Biscotti

If your idea of a biscotti is not-too-sweet, deeply chocolate, and crunchy with toasty almonds, this recipe is for you. Bittersweet chocolate chips are slightly less sweet than semisweet chocolate chips because of a higher percentage of cacao in them. So when they are melted and stirred into this dough, they provide more pronounced dark chocolate flavor.

½ cup bittersweet chocolate chips, divided
2 tablespoons unsalted butter
½ cup all-purpose flour
2 tablespoons unsweetened cocoa powder
¼ teaspoon baking soda
Pinch of salt
¼ cup sugar
Yolk of 1 large egg
¼ teaspoon pure vanilla extract
¼ teaspoon pure almond extract
14 dark chocolate–covered almonds, halved lengthwise, such as Dove

Position a rack in the center of the oven and preheat the oven to 350°F. Line a baking sheet with parchment paper and set it aside.

Place ¼ cup of the chocolate chips and the butter in a small microwave-safe bowl; microwave on medium power until the butter melts and the chocolate is soft, about 1 minute. Stir the chocolate mixture until it is smooth; let it cool 10 minutes.

Place the flour, cocoa powder, baking soda, and salt in a small, deep mixing bowl and whisk to blend.

Stir the sugar into the cooled chocolate mixture. Add the egg yolk and the vanilla and almond extracts, and whisk to blend. Add the chocolate mixture to the flour mixture, mixing well with a wooden spoon. Mix in the halved dark chocolate–covered almonds. The dough will be soft. Scrape the dough into the center of the bowl, cover, and refrigerate until it is firm enough to work with, about 30 minutes.

Lightly flour a work surface, and flour your hands. Transfer the dough to the work surface and form it into a 6 × 2 × 1-inch log. Place the log on the prepared baking sheet. Bake the log until it has risen and spread to about double its size and is dry when lightly touched, about 20 minutes.

Remove the baking sheet from the oven and gently transfer the log with a metal spatula to a wire rack to cool completely. Leave the parchment paper on the baking sheet. Turn the oven off.

When the log is cool, preheat the oven to 325°F.

Cut the cooled log diagonally with a serrated knife into eight slices, slicing a little off the ends to get even slices. Arrange the slices, cut sides down, on the parchment paper–lined baking sheet and bake until they are dry and golden brown, 12 to 15 minutes.

Remove the baking sheet from the oven and, using a thin spatula, turn the biscotti over. Return the biscotti to the oven and continue baking until they are dry, about 12 minutes. Remove the baking sheet from the oven and slide the parchment paper onto a wire rack. Let the biscotti cool completely.

Place the remaining ¼ cup chocolate chips in a small microwave-safe bowl; microwave on medium power until it is soft, about 1½ minutes. Stir until smooth. Spoon and spread the melted chocolate over one side of each biscotti, and refrigerate until the chocolate hardens, about 30 minutes.

Makes 8 biscotti

Bittersweet Chocolate Biscotti

This crisp, not too sweet, all-chocolate cookie is great with coffee. Make them the night before and store them in an airtight container. I like them better the next day; they seem to be more sturdy and better dunkers.

½ cup all-purpose flour
2 tablespoons unsweetened cocoa powder
¼ teaspoon baking powder
Pinch of salt
3 ounces fine-quality bittersweet chocolate, divided, finely chopped
2 tablespoons unsalted butter
¼ cup sugar
White of 1 large egg
½ teaspoon pure vanilla extract

Position a rack in the center of the oven and preheat the oven to 350°F. Line a baking sheet with parchment paper and set it aside.

Place the flour, cocoa powder, baking powder, and salt in a small, deep mixing bowl and whisk to blend.

Place 1 ounce of the finely chopped bittersweet chocolate and the butter in a small microwave-safe bowl; microwave on medium power until the chocolate is soft and the butter is melted, about 1 minute. Stir the chocolate mixture until it is smooth, then stir in the sugar. Add the egg white and the vanilla and whisk to blend. Add the chocolate mixture to the flour mixture, mixing well with a wooden spoon. Mix in the remaining 2 ounces of chopped bittersweet chocolate; the dough will be soft. Scrape the dough into the center of the bowl, cover, and refrigerate until it is firm enough to work with, about 30 minutes.

Lightly flour a work surface, and flour your hands. Transfer the dough to the work surface and form it into a 4½ × 2½ × 1½-inch log. Place the log on the prepared baking sheet. Bake until it is firm, about 20 minutes.

Remove the baking sheet from the oven and gently transfer the log with a metal spatula to a wire rack to cool completely. Leave the parchment paper on the baking sheet. Turn the oven off.

When the log is cool, preheat the oven to 325°F.

Cut the cooled log diagonally with a serrated knife into eight slices. Arrange them, cut sides down, on the parchment paper–lined baking sheet and bake until they are dry and golden brown, 12 to 15 minutes.

Remove the baking sheet from the oven and, using a thin spatula, turn the biscotti over. Continue baking until they are slightly dry, about 12 minutes. Remove the baking sheet from the oven and slide the parchment paper onto a wire rack. Let biscotti cool completely.

8 biscotti

&

OOEY-GOOEY GOODNESS
Luscious Puddings and Soufflés

❧

*P*uddings light and airy, creamy and rich, silky and velvety are in this section. If your occasion calls for sophistication and a less-than-heavy dessert, the White Chocolate Lemon Crème Brûlée, Chocolate Orange Flan, or Chocolate Raspberry Pots de Crème are perfect picks. To serve with Asian-inspired meals, or just to show off a unique flavor pairing with chocolate, the Wasabi Ginger Dark Chocolate Soufflé Puddings are the bomb.

Small-batch soufflés rise up high and puffy, making a spectacular impression. They are just right for a romantic mood because you will not leave the table too full for *après*-dinner activities. Most have homemade dessert sauces that are spooned into the centers of the soufflés for extra decadence.

For several years, I have been collecting pottery bowls to bake bread puddings in. When I go to an art show, a festival, or an artisan's shop, I go straight to the bowls, seeking out that special one that I can cup in my hands for warmth. Ovenproof latte cups are just the right size and shape to cook bread puddings in, too.

Mint Brownie Pudding Cakes

You have heard of wanting to do a face-plant into a bowlful of something yummy? This would be the bowl. A fudgy, minty cake layer separates from the pudding layer as it bakes, and the mints melt into the layers to give them crème de menthe flavor. I like to bake this in my deep cereal bowls, then curl up on the couch with a big spoon, a good book, and a soft blanket.

> ¼ cup all-purpose flour
>
> ¼ cup granulated sugar
>
> 3 tablespoons plus 1 teaspoon unsweetened cocoa powder, divided
>
> ⅛ teaspoon baking powder
>
> Pinch of salt
>
> 2 tablespoons well-beaten egg
>
> 2 tablespoons chocolate milk or milk
>
> 1½ tablespoons unsalted butter, melted and cooled
>
> ½ teaspoon pure vanilla extract
>
> ⅓ cup chopped crème de menthe chocolate mints, such as Andes,
>   about 10 mints
>
> 3 tablespoons firmly packed light brown sugar
>
> ⅓ cup boiling water
>
> Mint chocolate chip ice cream, optional

Position a rack in the center of the oven and preheat the oven to 350°F. Place two 1-cup ramekins or custard cups or two deep 1½- to 2-cup ovenproof bowls on a baking sheet for easier handling and set it aside.

Place the flour, granulated sugar, 2 tablespoons of the cocoa powder, baking powder, and salt in a medium bowl and whisk to blend.

Place the beaten egg, milk, butter, and vanilla in a small bowl, and whisk to blend. Pour the egg mixture over the flour mixture, and stir with a wooden spoon just until the batter is combined. Stir in the chopped chocolate mints. Spoon the batter into the ramekins, dividing it evenly.

Place the remaining 1 tablespoon plus 1 teaspoon cocoa powder, the brown sugar, and the boiling water in a small bowl and whisk to mix well. Pour the mixture over the batter in the ramekins. Bake the cakes until a toothpick inserted in the center of the top half of one of the cakes comes out with a few crumbs clinging to it, about 25 minutes. Remove the baking sheet from the oven, transfer the ramekins to a wire rack, and let them cool 10 minutes. Serve the cakes warm, in the ramekins, topped with scoops of ice cream, if using.

Makes 2 pudding cakes

Chocolate Peanut Soufflés with Peanut Butter Custard Sauce

One of my weaknesses is peanut butter. I eat it straight, with a spoon, and I went through so much of it when I was pregnant with my first child that she blames me for her peanut allergy. (Possibly rightly so.) One of my cats' names is Peanut. You understand . . .

When I considered how to make this ultimate chocolate soufflé even better, naturally I considered this princely pair. The sauce is so good you will be tempted to eat it by the spoonful.

> 2 teaspoons unsalted butter for greasing the soufflé dishes
> 2 teaspoons unsweetened cocoa powder, divided
> ¼ cup chocolate milk
> 2 large egg yolks
> 1 teaspoon all-purpose flour
> Pinch of salt
> 2 ounces fine-quality milk chocolate, chopped
> ½ teaspoon pure vanilla extract
> 2 large egg whites
> 2 tablespoons sugar
> 3 tablespoons chopped honey-roasted or cocktail peanuts
> Peanut Butter Custard Sauce (recipe follows)

Position a rack in the center of the oven and preheat the oven to 350°F.

Butter the insides of two 8-ounce soufflé dishes or ramekins; dust the insides with 1 teaspoon cocoa powder and tap out the excess. Make collars for the soufflé dishes: cut two bands of aluminum foil and fold over to make them double-thickness, 4 inches wide, and long enough to go around the dishes, allowing 3 inches of the foil bands to overlap. Wrap the collars around the outsides of the dishes and fasten around the dishes with string. The collars should extend 2 to 3 inches above the rim of the dish. Place the prepared soufflé dishes on a baking sheet for easier handling and set aside.

Whisk the chocolate milk, egg yolks, flour, 1 teaspoon of cocoa powder, and salt in a small saucepan until well blended. Place over medium-low heat and cook, stirring constantly, until the mixture is thickened, about 5 minutes. Remove from the heat; add the chopped chocolate and stir until the chocolate melts and the mixture is smooth. Stir in the vanilla. Let cool to room temperature.

Place the egg whites and 2 tablespoons sugar in a small, deep mixing bowl and beat with a handheld electric mixer until firm peaks form. Fold one-fourth of the egg whites into the chocolate mixture; fold the chocolate mixture into the remaining egg whites. Spoon the mixture into the soufflé dishes. Sprinkle with the peanuts, dividing them evenly. Bake until the soufflés are set, 23 to 26 minutes. To serve, place each soufflé dish on a napkin-lined serving plate. Serve immediately with the Peanut Butter Custard Sauce.

Makes 2 souffles

Peanut Butter Custard Sauce
¼ cup whole milk
¼ cup half-and-half
1 large egg yolk
1½ tablespoons sugar
1 teaspoon all-purpose flour
3 tablespoons smooth peanut butter

Pour the milk and half-and-half into a small, heavy saucepan. Bring it to a simmer over medium-high heat.

Place the egg yolk, sugar, and flour in a small bowl; whisk to blend well. Gradually whisk some of the hot milk mixture into the eggs; whisk the egg mixture into the remaining hot milk mixture in the saucepan. Bring to a simmer, whisking constantly. Simmer, stirring, until thickened. Remove from the heat and whisk in the peanut butter.

Transfer the custard sauce to a small bowl; place that bowl in a larger bowl filled with ice. Let the sauce cool until thickened and chilled, stirring occasionally.

Makes about ¾ cup

Chocolate Chip Cookie Soufflés

Many of these recipes get their unique character from my daughter's and her friends' suggestions. We do a lot of small-batch baking in my house; the girls love mini-cooking lessons when they visit. One day we were having an egg-separating lesson with this soufflé, and the friend suggested we crumble cookies on them before baking. Eleni took it one step further and suggested chocolate chips on top. Presto! A recipe was born!

2 teaspoons unsalted butter for greasing the soufflé dishes

2 tablespoons plus 1 teaspoon sugar, divided

1½ ounces semisweet chocolate, chopped

½ ounce unsweetened chocolate, chopped

¼ cup heavy (whipping) cream

1 large egg yolk

Pinch of salt

2 large egg whites

¼ cup crumbled Brownie Cookies (page 130) or other chocolate chip cookies (2 to 3 cookies)

3 tablespoons semisweet chocolate chips

Position a rack in the center of the oven and preheat the oven to 350°F. Use the 2 teaspoons butter to butter the insides of two 8-ounce soufflé dishes or ramekins; sprinkle the insides with 1 teaspoon of the sugar and tap out the excess. Make collars for the soufflé dishes: cut two bands of aluminum foil and fold each over to make them double-thickness, 4 inches wide, and long enough to go around the dishes, allowing 3 inches of the foil bands to overlap. Wrap the collars around the outsides of the dishes and fasten around the dishes with string. The collars should extend 2 to 3 inches above the rim of the dishes. Place the prepared soufflé dishes on a baking sheet for easier handling and set aside.

Place the chocolate in a microwave-safe bowl; microwave on medium power until soft, about 1 minute. Stir until smooth. Whisk in the cream, then the egg yolk and salt.

Place the egg whites and remaining 2 tablespoons sugar in a small, deep mixing bowl and beat with a handheld electric mixer until firm peaks form, about 1½ minutes. Stir one-fourth of the egg whites into the chocolate mixture; fold the chocolate mixture into the remaining egg whites. Spoon the mixture into the soufflé dishes. Sprinkle the crumbled cookies and the chocolate chips over the soufflés. Bake until a toothpick inserted in the centers comes out clean, 21 to 23 minutes. Serve immediately.

Makes 2 souffles

Chocolate Earl Grey Tea Soufflés

I like the sophisticated flavor of this combination, and the ease with which they are made. Once the chocolate, tea-flavored custard sauce is made, a portion of it is reserved for the finishing sauce and the rest is folded into egg whites and baked.

Earl Grey's distinctive fragrance comes from the oil in the rind of bergamot citrus. Because it is a black tea, you can use that in this recipe, too.

1 teaspoon unsalted butter, for preparing the soufflé dishes

1 teaspoon sugar, for preparing the soufflé dishes

2 large eggs, separated

1 large egg yolk

¼ cup plus 2 teaspoons sugar, divided

½ teaspoon cornstarch

Pinch of salt

1 cup milk

4 Earl Grey or black tea bags

1½ ounces bittersweet chocolate, chopped

½ ounce unsweetened chocolate, chopped

Position a rack in the center of the oven and preheat the oven to 350°F.

Make collars for two 8-ounce soufflé dishes or ramekins: cut two bands of aluminum foil and fold over to make them 4 inches wide and long enough to go around the dishes, allowing the foil to wrap all the way around and overlap at the ends. Wrap the collars around the outsides of the dishes, and secure with string. The collars should extend 2 to 3 inches above the rims of the dishes.

Use the 1 teaspoon butter to butter the insides of the soufflé dishes and the insides of the collars; sprinkle the insides with 1 teaspoon of the sugar and tap out the excess. Place the prepared soufflé dishes on a baking sheet for easier handling and set it aside.

Have ready a medium bowl of ice and water for cooling the custard.

Place the 3 egg yolks, 2 teaspoons of sugar, cornstarch, and salt in a small mixing bowl; whisk the mixture until the sugar and cornstarch dissolve.

Place the milk, tea bags, and 3 tablespoons of the sugar in a small saucepan. Bring to a simmer over medium heat, stirring until the sugar dissolves. Cover, remove from the heat, and let it stand 5 minutes to brew the tea. Lift out the tea bags, pressing them gently to extract the liquid from them.

Add the chocolates to the milk mixture, and stir until the custard is smooth. Measure out ¼ cup of the custard; cover and set the sauce aside for serving the soufflés.

Pour the remaining custard mixture into a bowl; place in the ice water bath and let it cool to room temperature, stirring the custard occasionally.

Place the 2 egg whites and the remaining 1 tablespoon of the sugar in a small, deep mixing bowl and beat with a handheld electric mixer until firm peaks form, about 1½ minutes. Gently fold the cooled custard mixture, in 3 batches, into the beaten egg whites until no streaks of white remain. Pour into the prepared soufflé dishes, dividing it evenly between them. Bake until puffed and set, about 30 minutes.

To serve, carefully place the soufflé dishes on napkin-lined serving plates; cut the string and gently peel off the collars. Dip a tablespoon into the centers of the soufflés and pour in the custard sauce, dividing it evenly between the soufflés.

Makes 2 soufflés

∽

Wasabi Ginger Dark Chocolate Soufflé Puddings

Chocolate pairs uniquely with many savory flavors. This was an experiment that turned out spectacularly well; there is heat from both the wasabi and the ginger, much like chili pepper when it is added to a chocolate dessert. If you want a more simple chocolate version, you can leave out the wasabi, the ginger, or both to change up this velvety soufflé and the crème anglaise.

> ¼ cup plus 3 tablespoons whole milk
> 1 teaspoon grated fresh ginger with juice
> ½ teaspoon wasabi powder
> ¼ cup plus 1 tablespoon sugar, divided
> 1 tablespoon all-purpose flour
> 2 ounces bittersweet chocolate, chopped
> 2 teaspoons unsalted butter or margarine, plus butter for greasing
>   the ramekins
> 1 large egg, separated
> Wasabi Ginger Crème Anglaise (recipe follows)

Place a rack in the center of the oven and preheat the oven to 325°F. Lightly butter two 1-cup capacity ramekins, and place them in a square baking pan. Set the pan aside.

Whisk together the milk, ginger, and wasabi powder in a small saucepan. Cook over medium heat until the mixture simmers, stirring occasionally,

3 to 4 minutes. Pour through a fine-mesh sieve to remove the ginger particles, pressing on the solids. Return the liquid to the saucepan.

Whisk in 3 tablespoons of the sugar and the flour. Add the chocolate and 2 teaspoons butter, stirring until melted and smooth. Whisk the egg yolk in a small bowl; gradually beat in a little of the hot chocolate mixture. Whisk the egg yolk mixture back into the saucepan. Cook over medium-low heat, stirring constantly, until the custard mixture is thickened and coats the back of a spoon, about 5 minutes; when a finger is drawn down the back of the spoon, the space does not fill in with custard mixture.

Beat the egg white and the remaining 2 tablespoons of sugar in a small mixing bowl until firm peaks form. Gently and gradually whisk in the chocolate mixture and spoon the mixture into the prepared ramekins. Bake until puffed and set, about 25 minutes. Remove the baking pan from the oven; lift the puddings out of the pan with a flat, slotted spatula. Place on napkin-lined serving plates. To serve, make a well in the middle of each soufflé using a dessert spoon, and spoon some of the Wasabi Ginger Crème Anglaise into the center.

Makes 2 puddings

Wasabi Ginger Crème Anglaise
1½ tablespoons beaten egg yolk (about 1½ large egg yolks)
2 tablespoons sugar
¼ cup plus 3 tablespoons half-and-half
½ teaspoon grated fresh ginger and juice
¼ teaspoon wasabi powder
1 ounce bittersweet chocolate, finely chopped

Whisk the egg yolks and sugar in a small mixing bowl until the mixture is pale in color, about 1 minute.

Whisk together the half-and-half, ginger, and wasabi in a medium saucepan; bring to a boil, whisking constantly. Pour through a fine-mesh sieve into a bowl to remove the ginger particles, pressing on the solids.

Gradually pour one-fourth of the hot half-and-half mixture over the beaten egg yolk mixture, whisking constantly. Whisk in the remaining hot half-and-half mixture. Pour back into the saucepan, scraping the bowl with a rubber spatula. Cook the custard sauce over medium-low heat, whisking gently and constantly, until the mixture coats back of a spoon, about 8 minutes.

Place a clean bowl in a larger bowl of ice and water. Pour the crème anglaise through the fine-mesh sieve into the clean bowl. Let the custard sauce cool to room temperature over the ice water bath, whisking gently and occasionally as it cools. Cover and store in the refrigerator up to 4 hours. Serve chilled.

Makes ⅔ cup

Hot Chocolate Chip Bread Pudding with Brandy Sauce

This is a traditional bread pudding with brandy sauce, but the smooth chocolate custard and the chips folded into the pudding make it better than ever.

> ¾ cup whole or chocolate milk (not lowfat)
> ⅔ cup (4 ounces) semisweet chocolate chips, divided
> 1 large egg
> 2 tablespoons sugar
> Pinch of salt
> 1 teaspoon pure vanilla extract
> 2 cups day-old egg bread cubes (1-inch cubes)
> Brandy Sauce (recipe follows)

Position a rack in the center of the oven and preheat the oven to 350°F. Lightly butter two 1-cup ramekins or custard cups; place them on a baking sheet for easier handling and set it aside.

Pour the milk into a small saucepan and bring it to a boil over medium-high heat. Remove the pan from the heat and add ⅓ cup of the chocolate chips, swirling the pan to immerse the chocolate in the milk. Let it stand 1 minute; stir until smooth.

Place the egg, sugar, salt, and vanilla in a medium bowl and whisk until the mixture is frothy, about 20 seconds. Continue whisking while you gradually pour in the chocolate cream. Add the bread, pressing down on it with a spatula to submerge it. Let the mixture stand, pressing on the bread occasionally to keep it submerged, until the bread is saturated and the mixture is room temperature, about 30 minutes. Stir in the remaining ⅓ cup chocolate chips.

Spoon the mixture into the prepared ramekins, dividing it evenly between them. Bake until the puddings are just set, about 30 minutes.

Remove the baking sheet from the oven; transfer the ramekins to a wire rack, and let them cool 10 minutes while you make the Brandy Sauce.

Invert the warm bread puddings onto serving plates, and spoon the Brandy Sauce over them.

Makes 2 puddings

Brandy Sauce

This sauce is called a sabayon, a foamy egg-thickened sauce. The egg yolks are beaten with sugar in a bowl set over, but not touching, simmering water. For extra fluff, the cooled custard is folded into whipped cream.

2 large egg yolks
2 tablespoons sugar
¼ cup plus 2 tablespoons heavy (whipping) cream, divided
1 tablespoon brandy
½ teaspoon pure vanilla extract

Fit a small metal bowl snugly in a small saucepan; pour enough water in the saucepan to stay below the bottom of the bowl by 1 inch, and bring it to a simmer. Fill a larger bowl with ice and water, and set it aside for cooling the sauce.

Place the egg yolks and sugar in the metal bowl. Whisk in 2 tablespoons of the cream and the brandy. Set the bowl over the saucepan of simmering water (do not let the bottom of the bowl touch the water) and cook, whisking constantly, until the mixture is thickened, 4 to 5 minutes. When you drag a spoon across the bottom of the bowl, it should leave a trail of uncovered pan that lingers before the sauce fills it in.

Remove the bowl from the simmering water and place it in the larger bowl of ice water. Stir in the vanilla. Let the custard mixture cool, stirring it gently with a rubber spatula, until it is chilled.

Place the remaining ¼ cup of cream in a small, deep mixing bowl and beat with a handheld electric mixer on high speed until firm peaks form, about 1¼ minutes. Gently but thoroughly fold the whipped cream into the custard mixture. Use the sabayon immediately or refrigerate it up to 1 hour before serving.

Makes about ⅔ cup

Chai Custard Bread Pudding

Spice blends have, up until recently, been up to the individual cook to put together from several bottles to achieve the proper balance of flavors. Now, several large spice companies do that for us. I love to take advantage of them; they are convenient to use and it is less expensive to purchase one bottle of a blend rather than many.

Take this chai spice blend, for instance. The traditional cinnamon, cardamom, ginger, and other warm spices are in perfect proportion to infuse the delicate custard that soaks thin layers of bread. The melted chocolate chip layer on the bottom forms a saucy chocolate layer.

1 tablespoon unsalted butter, softened

4 slices Pepperidge Farm white bread, crusts removed

1 large egg

1 large egg yolk

1 tablespoon sugar plus 2 teaspoons sugar for caramelizing, divided

¾ cup half-and-half

½ teaspoon pure vanilla extract

½ teaspoon chai spice blend, such as McCormick

Pinch of salt

⅓ cup (2 ounces) semisweet chocolate chips

Position a rack in the center of the oven and preheat the oven to 350°F. Lightly butter two 1-cup capacity custard cups or ramekins; place them in an 8- or 9-inch baking pan and set the pan aside.

Spread the butter on one side of each piece of bread. Cut the bread slices on the diagonal into eight equal-size triangles.

Place the egg, egg yolk, and 1 tablespoon sugar in a medium bowl and whisk to beat the egg. Add the half-and-half, vanilla, chai spice blend, and salt; whisk until well blended.

In each prepared ramekin, sprinkle half of the chocolate chips on the bottom. Arrange 4 bread triangles in a single layer on top of the chocolate, fitting them together to re-form a slice. Sprinkle with another layer of chocolate chips and bread. Repeat the layers.

Pour the custard mixture over the bread, dividing it evenly between the custard cups. Press the bread down to make sure the custard is soaked up by the bread. Pour enough hot water into the baking pan to come halfway up the sides of the cups. Bake until the puddings are just set and a knife inserted in the centers comes out clean, 33 to 35 minutes.

Remove the puddings from the oven; transfer the ramekins to a wire rack to cool 10 minutes. Sprinkle 1 teaspoon sugar over each bread pudding; caramelize with a kitchen blowtorch or place the puddings under the broiler until the sugar caramelizes, about 1 minute.

Makes 2 puddings

❦

Caramel-Topped Bread Pudding

Made from French bread, which is not as dense as others, this pudding is light in texture, with a very chocolate custard. Served with the Rich Caramel Sauce and toasted pecans, it's got candy bar flavors in a delicious dessert.

⅔ cup chocolate milk (not lowfat)

⅔ semisweet chocolate chips, divided

1 large egg

1 tablespoon sugar

1 teaspoon pure vanilla extract

1½ cups day-old French bread cubes (1-inch cubes)

¼ cup Rich Caramel Sauce (page 244) or store-bought caramel
   sundae syrup

¼ cup chopped pecans, lightly toasted or unsalted
   dry-roasted peanuts

Position a rack in the center of the oven and preheat the oven to 350°F. Lightly butter two 1-cup ramekins or custard cups; place them on a baking sheet for easier handling and set it aside.

Pour the milk into a small saucepan and bring it to a boil over medium-high heat. Remove the pan from the heat and add ⅓ cup of the chocolate chips, swirling the pan to immerse the chocolate in the milk. Let it stand 1 minute; stir until smooth.

Place the egg, sugar, and vanilla in a medium bowl and whisk until the mixture is frothy, about 20 seconds. Continue whisking while you gradually pour in the chocolate cream. Add the bread, pressing down on it with a spatula to submerge it. Let the mixture stand, pressing on the bread occasionally to keep it submerged, until the bread is saturated, about 10 minutes.

Spoon the mixture into the prepared ramekins, dividing it evenly between them. Bake until the puddings are just set, 30 to 35 minutes. Remove the baking sheet from the oven. Sprinkle the remaining ⅓ cup chocolate chips on top of the puddings. Drizzle the caramel sauce over the puddings and sprinkle them with the pecans. Return the baking sheet to the oven and bake until the caramel syrup is bubbling, about 1 minute.

Remove the baking sheet from the oven; transfer the ramekins to a wire rack, and let them cool 10 minutes. Serve them warm in their ramekins.

Makes 2 servings

White Chocolate Lemon Crème Brûlée

My husband has a weakness for lemon desserts. I bought two shallow crème brûlée dishes—heart-shaped—to make this for him; the custard with its caramelized sugar top is just beautiful baked and served in them. They are pretty garnished with small lavender sprigs and slices of candied lemon. (See page 282 for Candied Oranges, and substitute lemon slices in the recipe.)

    1 cup heavy (whipping) cream
    1 tablespoon finely grated lemon zest
    1 ounce fine-quality white chocolate, chopped
    2½ tablespoons beaten egg yolks (about 2½ large egg yolks)
    3 tablespoons sugar plus 2 teaspoons sugar for caramelizing, divided
    2 teaspoons freshly squeezed lemon juice
    1 teaspoon vanilla extract
    Pinch of salt

Position a rack in the center of the oven and preheat the oven to 325°F. Place two 5 × 1-inch round crème brûlée dishes or similar-size ramekins in a large baking pan for easier handling and set it aside.

Place the cream and lemon zest in a small, heavy saucepan; bring to a boil. Cover, reduce the heat, and simmer 1 minute. Remove from the heat. Pour through a fine-mesh sieve into a bowl, and discard the lemon zest. Add the white chocolate; stir until smooth.

Meanwhile, whisk the egg yolks and 3 tablespoons of sugar together until blended in a bowl. While you are continuing to whisk, gradually pour in the hot milk mixture. Whisk in the lemon juice, vanilla, and salt.

Strain through a fine-mesh sieve into the dishes, dividing it evenly. Put the pan into the oven, and carefully pour enough hot water into the baking pan to come halfway up the sides of the dishes.

Bake until the custards are just set but still slightly jiggly, 26 to 30 minutes. Carefully remove the dishes from the hot water in the baking pan. Transfer them to a wire rack and let them cool slightly. Cover and refrigerate until cold, about 6 hours or overnight.

Just before serving, preheat the broiler. Sprinkle the tops of the crème brûlées with 1 teaspoon sugar each. Place under the broiler until the sugar is caramelized, 3 to 4 minutes, or caramelize the sugar with a kitchen torch.

Makes 2 servings

ᕦᕤ

Chocolate Raspberry Pots de Crème

Traditionally, this dessert was a lightly set custard that was baked and served in small cups because they were too liquid to be unmolded—like flan, for instance. The cups and the custard are referred to as *"pots de crème,"* or "pots of cream." The small cups, or pots, have tiny "teapot" lids, are made of porcelain, and hold about 3 ounces of custard.

My pots de crème set is still in a box somewhere in the basement from this year's move, so I bake these in custard cups instead.

1 ounce bittersweet chocolate, chopped
¼ ounce unsweetened chocolate, chopped
1 cup heavy (whipping) cream
1½ tablespoons beaten egg yolk (about 1½ large egg yolks)
2 tablespoons sugar
1 tablespoon unsweetened cocoa powder
1 tablespoon Chambord or other raspberry-flavored liqueur
1 teaspoon pure vanilla extract
Pinch of salt
Sweetened whipped cream
Fresh raspberries

Position a rack in the center of the oven and preheat the oven to 300°F. Place two 6-ounce custard cups or decorative bowls in an 8- or 9-inch square baking pan and set the pan aside.

Place the chocolates in a small bowl. Place the cream in a small, heavy saucepan; bring to a simmer. Remove the pan from the heat and pour about ⅓ cup of the hot cream over the chocolates in the bowl; let stand 1 minute and stir until smooth. Scrape the chocolate mixture into the saucepan of the remaining hot cream; whisk gently to blend.

Place the beaten egg yolks in another small bowl. Pour a little of the hot cream mixture into the egg yolks, whisking constantly; whisk the egg yolk mixture back into the saucepan of the hot cream mixture.

Whisk the sugar and cocoa together in a small bowl; pour into the hot cream mixture. Cook over low heat, stirring constantly, until the mixture is thickened and coats the back of a spoon, about 5 minutes. Remove from the heat and stir in the liqueur, vanilla, and salt.

Pour the mixture into the custard cups. Pour enough hot water into the baking pan to come halfway up the sides of the cups. Bake until the custards are softly set but still jiggly, 30 to 35 minutes.

Carefully remove the custard cups from the water in the baking pan, lifting them carefully out of the water with a flat, slotted metal spatula. Place in the refrigerator, uncovered, until they are cool. Then cover with plastic wrap and refrigerate until cold, about 6 hours or overnight.

Serve topped with whipped cream; garnish with fresh raspberries.

Makes 2 pots de crème

Mocha Pots de Crème

This variation is for coffee lovers. Adding a little espresso and chocolate liqueur to the custard gives it rich mocha flavor. Garnish the desserts with whipped cream and Chocolate Curls (page 31).

Prepare Chocolate Raspberry Pots de Crème as the recipe directs, except stir ½ teaspoon of espresso powder or instant coffee powder into the hot cream until it is dissolved. Substitute 1 tablespoon Kahlúa or other coffee liqueur for the Chambord or other raspberry liqueur.

BODACIOUS BREADS
Melt-in-Your-Mouth Muffins, Scones, Shortcakes, and Loaves

∽

*T*his is my happy chapter. I definitely bake more small batches of scones and muffins in the morning than I would if I were baking a dozen or more of them. That wake-up call is soothing and fragrant, and no matter which side of the bed I've climbed out of, one of these warm, moist breads will always start the day off right.

You will find some chocolate in every one of these quick breads, sometimes subtle but mostly in-your-face. For instance, there is nothing measly about the chocolate flavor in Coffee Shop Chocolate Muffins, but what a difference a little grated chocolate makes in the Happy Morning Muffins! The Java Choco Banana Muffins would not taste quite right without the meltingly gooey chips. Even the best banana bread recipe could not compete with Whole Wheat Chocolate Banana Bread; adding grated chocolate makes the bread ultramoist and gives it wonderful flavor.

And, aahhh, the scones! Just try Rich Sweet Vanilla Chocolate Chip Scones on your significant other one morning . . . Bake the Pumpkin Spice White Chocolate Scones during the fall; they send warm spice aromas through the kitchen, and nothing (except coffee, maybe) says "good morning" better during cold weather. For everyday luxury, the Oatmeal Chocolate Chip Scones add just the right amount of healthy oats to make you feel righteous.

The little loaves of chocolate bread in this chapter are the perfect solutions to a sweet ending for brunch or a bite to go with your afternoon tea or coffee; they also make great little gifts if you want something easy but fabulous to bake.

When you are looking for a quick and easy dessert that is richly chocolate, try one of the shortcakes in this chapter. Milk chocolate is grated and mixed into the flaky dough for Milk Chocolate Shortcakes, and the Banana Split Shortcakes are all chocolate, with chips, too. They both have homemade sauces serving suggestions that will satisfy your sweet tooth, and make you wonder why you would ever buy store-bought chocolate or caramel sauce again.

Chocolate Tea Loaf

I love this for a simple breakfast with a cup of coffee and some fruit. I can make a loaf one day and it will keep well for several days, if it lasts that long. The bread is ultramoist with the cooled spiked sugar syrup soaked through the loaf. Let it cool completely and even chill it before you slice it; it will hold its shape better.

    ⅔ cup all-purpose flour
    ½ teaspoon baking powder
    ⅛ teaspoon baking soda
    ⅛ teaspoon salt
    ¼ cup unsalted butter, softened
    ¼ cup plus 2 tablespoons sugar
    1 ounce unsweetened chocolate, melted and cooled
    ½ teaspoon pure vanilla extract
    2½ tablespoons well-beaten egg
    2 tablespoons sour cream
    ⅓ cup semisweet chocolate chips
    Sugar Syrup (recipe follows)

Position a rack in the center of the oven and preheat the oven to 350°F. Lightly spray the inside of a petite loaf pan (2-cup capacity, about 5 × 3 inches) with cooking spray; line the bottom of the pan lengthwise and up the short ends with a strip of parchment paper, allowing the ends to extend 1½ inches above the edges. Set the pan aside.

Place the flour, baking powder, baking soda, and salt in a bowl; whisk to blend the dry ingredients.

Place the butter and sugar in a small, deep mixing bowl. Beat with a hand-held electric mixer on high speed until light and fluffy, about 1 minute. Beat in the cooled chocolate and vanilla. Beat in the egg and sour cream on low speed. Add the flour mixture, and beat on low speed just until the dry ingredients are moistened. Fold in the chocolate chips. Spoon into the prepared pan. Bake until a toothpick inserted in the center of the bread comes out clean, about 40 minutes. Place on a wire rack. Poke holes all over the top of the bread with a long skewer; pour the syrup over the cake. Let it cool completely in the pan. Remove from the pan and cool completely before slicing. (The cake will keep 2 days in an airtight container.)

Makes 1 loaf, 4 to 5 slices

Sugar Syrup
2 tablespoons water
1½ tablespoons sugar
1 tablespoon chocolate liqueur, optional

Place the water and sugar in a small microwave-safe bowl; microwave on high power 2 minutes, stirring after 30 seconds. Let cool to room temperature and stir in the liqueur, if using.

Makes about 3½ tablespoons

൭

Chocolate Cherry Bread

On Valentine's Day, for many years, my dad gave me a small box of chocolate-covered cherries, which we happily shared. This bread brings back wonderful memories of treats we loved.

If you use fresh cherries, they will be firmer after baking; frozen cherries will give it great flavor, but they will bake up softer. The fruit and sour cream work together to keep the loaf moist, and it will keep nicely in the refrigerator for a couple of days if you wrap it tightly in plastic wrap.

> 20 fresh or frozen, pitted, sweet cherries (about 1 cup)
> ½ cup plus 2 tablespoons all-purpose flour
> 2 tablespoons unsweetened cocoa powder
> ½ teaspoon baking powder
> ⅛ teaspoon baking soda
> ⅛ teaspoon salt
> ¼ cup plus 2 tablespoons sugar
> 2 tablespoons sour cream
> 3 tablespoons well-beaten egg
> 2 tablespoons unsalted butter, melted and cooled

If you are using frozen cherries, place them in a colander over a bowl and let them thaw completely and drain. Reserve the juices for another use. Cut ten of the fresh or thawed, frozen cherries into quarters and set them aside. Drain the thawed, frozen cherries again before using them in the batter.

Position a rack in the center of the oven and preheat the oven to 350°F. Lightly spray the inside of a petite loaf pan (2-cup capacity, about 5 × 3 inches) with cooking spray. Line the bottom of the pan lengthwise and up the short ends with a strip of parchment paper, allowing the edges to extend 1½ inches above the edges. Set the pan aside.

Place the flour, cocoa powder, baking powder, baking soda, and salt in a bowl; whisk to blend.

Place the remaining whole cherries, the sugar, sour cream, egg, and butter in a food processor bowl; process until the cherries are pureed. Add to the flour mixture, along with the drained, quartered cherries, and stir just until the dry ingredients are moistened.

Bake until a toothpick inserted in the center of the bread comes out clean, about 40 minutes. Place on a wire rack to cool 15 minutes. Remove the loaf from the pan and cool completely before slicing.

Makes 5 slices

Chocolate Lime Bread

You may have doubts, but this combination tastes incredible. I stumbled on it while I was trying to make a thickened buttermilk-like mixture out of chocolate milk, knowing in my Southern baker's instincts that buttermilk makes a tender bread. I did not have lemon so I tried lime, and the flavor blew me away. It makes a nice loaf—not too sweet—to serve for brunch.

¼ cup plus 3½ tablespoons chocolate milk, divided

2 teaspoons freshly squeezed lime juice, divided

⅔ cup all-purpose flour

¼ cup sugar

1 tablespoon unsweetened cocoa powder

½ teaspoon baking powder

½ teaspoon baking soda

¼ teaspoon salt

½ teaspoon finely grated lime zest

2 tablespoons cold, unsalted butter, cut into bits

1 tablespoon well-beaten egg

½ cup confectioners' sugar

Position a rack in the center of the oven and preheat the oven to 425°F. Lightly spray the inside of a petite loaf pan (2-cup capacity, about 5 × 3 inches) with cooking spray. Line the bottom of the pan lengthwise and up the short ends with a strip of parchment paper, allowing the edges to extend 1½ inches above the edges. Set the pan aside.

Pour ¼ cup plus 2½ tablespoons of the chocolate milk into a glass measuring cup; stir in 1 teaspoon of the lime juice. Let stand at room temperature 10 minutes. The mixture may appear slightly curdled.

Place the flour, sugar, cocoa powder, baking powder, baking soda, salt, and lime zest in a medium bowl; whisk the dry ingredients to blend well. Add the butter and cut in with a pastry blender until coarse crumbs form.

Whisk the egg into the chocolate milk mixture. Add the chocolate milk mixture to the dry ingredients and stir just until combined. Pour into the prepared loaf pan. Bake until a toothpick inserted in the center comes out clean, 28 to 30 minutes.

Remove the loaf pan from the oven and let it cool on a wire rack for 10 minutes. Then remove the bread from the pan and let it cool upright on the rack.

Place the confectioners' sugar, remaining ½ tablespoon chocolate milk, and remaining 1 teaspoon lime juice in a small bowl, and stir it until very smooth. Add another ½ tablespoon of chocolate milk to thin it, if necessary. Poke six holes in the warm chocolate loaf, using a long skewer, all the way to the bottom of the pan; drizzle the glaze on top. Let it cool to room temperature. (The loaf may be wrapped in aluminum foil, placed in a freezer bag, and frozen up to 1 month.)

Makes 1 loaf, 4 to 5 slices.

ɷ

Chai Spice Chocolate Crumb Cakes

Tea and chai spices add subtle flavor to these individual crumb cakes. To make them, you put together dry ingredients and make a crumb mixture, saving some for the top, and adding wet ingredients and baking powder to the remainder to make the batter. Both the cakes and the topping have chocolate pieces in them.

  3 tablespoons whole milk
  1 black tea bag
  ½ cup plus 1½ tablespoons all-purpose flour
  1 ounce semisweet chocolate, finely chopped
  ¼ cup plus 1 tablespoon sugar
  ⅛ teaspoon ground cinnamon
  ⅛ teaspoon ground cardamom
  Pinch of ground cloves
  ⅛ teaspoon salt
  2½ tablespoons unsalted butter, cut into pieces, plus butter for the
    muffin cups
  ¼ teaspoon baking powder
  1½ tablespoons well-beaten egg

Position a rack in the center of the oven and preheat the oven to 375°F. Lightly butter and flour the bottoms (only) of three regular muffin cups (½-cup capacity) and rub a little butter around the rim of each cup. (This will help them to form a rounded top.) Set the muffin pan aside.

Pour the milk into a small microwave-safe bowl; add the tea bag. Microwave on high power for 20 seconds, or until simmering. Cover the bowl and let the tea steep for 5 minutes. Lift the tea bag from the milk, squeezing the bag gently with the back of a spoon against the side of the bowl to extract all the liquid.

Place the flour, chocolate, sugar, spices, and salt in a medium bowl; stir with a whisk to blend well. Add the butter and cut into the dry ingredients with a pastry blender until crumbly. Measure out and set aside 3 tablespoons of the crumb mixture for the topping.

Add the baking powder and the egg to the milk mixture; whisk until blended. Add to the remaining crumb mixture in the medium bowl and stir until a batter is formed.

Spoon the batter into the prepared muffin cups, dividing it evenly among them. Sprinkle the reserved crumb mixture evenly over the batter and press it in lightly with your fingertips. Fill the empty muffin cups halfway with water to prevent them from scorching.

Bake the cakes until a toothpick inserted in the center of one comes out clean, about 23 minutes.

Remove the muffin pan from the oven and place it on a wire rack to cool for 5 minutes. Carefully pour the water out of the empty muffin cups. Turn the cakes out of the cups and let them cool, upright, on the wire rack for at least 10 minutes before serving. Serve warm or at room temperature. (The cakes may be wrapped in aluminum foil, placed in a plastic freezer bag, and frozen for up to 1 month. Store any leftovers, wrapped at room temperature, for up to 2 days.)

Makes 3 crumb cakes

Coffee Shop Chocolate Muffins

I am a sucker for chocolate muffins, but those you can buy with your coffee or packaged in stores are usually high in fat, sugar, and calories. This homemade version is much more satisfying, since I know they are not loading me up with too much of anything except lovely chocolate flavor. They get tenderness from some sugar and butter, sure, but the buttermilk is an old Southern baking secret to moist, light texture.

¼ cup sugar

3 tablespoons unsalted butter, melted and cooled

3 tablespoons buttermilk

½ teaspoon pure vanilla extract

3 tablespoons well-beaten egg

⅓ cup plus 3 tablespoons all-purpose flour

1 tablespoon plus 1 teaspoon unsweetened cocoa powder

½ teaspoon baking powder

¼ teaspoon baking soda

⅛ teaspoon salt

½ cup semisweet chocolate chips

Position a rack in the center of the oven and preheat the oven to 350°F. Line two cups of a jumbo muffin pan (¾-cup capacity) with paper liners, or lightly butter the bottoms (only) of the cups and rub a little butter around the rim of each cup. (This will help them to form a rounded top.) Set the muffin pan aside.

Place the sugar, melted butter, buttermilk, vanilla, and egg in a small bowl and whisk to blend. Set aside.

Place a large, fine-mesh sieve over a medium bowl. Place the flour, cocoa powder, baking powder, baking soda, and salt in the sieve, and sift the ingredients into the bowl. Add the buttermilk mixture all at once and stir just until the dry ingredients are moistened. Stir in the chocolate chips. Spoon the batter into the prepared muffin cups, dividing it evenly between them. Fill the empty muffin cups halfway with water to prevent them from scorching. Bake the muffins until a toothpick inserted into the center of one comes out clean, 27 to 30 minutes.

Remove the muffin pan from the oven and place it on a wire rack to cool for 5 minutes. Carefully pour the water out of the empty muffin cups. Turn the muffins out of the cups and let them cool, upright, on the wire rack for at least 10 minutes before serving. Serve warm or at room temperature. (These are best eaten the day they are baked but will keep up to 1 day in a plastic bag at room temperature.)

Note: To make regular-size muffins, line four standard muffin cups with paper liners or butter the cups as directed above. Spoon the batter into the cups and bake as directed, 15 to 18 minutes.

Makes 2 jumbo-size muffins or 4 regular-size muffins

Granola Chocolate Chip Muffins

Some folks say that the people who live in my city (Asheville) are "granola." I take it as a compliment; it means that, as a whole, we are full of flavors and unique textures woven into a down-to-earth community. As are these muffins; there is not a bite among them that is missing sweet, tart, crunchy, and chewy.

For breakfast, I love to split them, warm from the oven, and slather them with peanut butter for a protein boost. Then I am ready for my morning workout, with energy left over.

½ cup plus 2 tablespoons all-purpose flour
¾ teaspoon baking powder
¼ teaspoon baking soda
⅛ teaspoon salt
Pinch of freshly grated nutmeg
½ cup granola without raisins, divided
¼ cup buttermilk
¼ cup firmly packed light brown sugar
2½ tablespoons well-beaten egg
2 tablespoons vegetable oil
½ teaspoon pure vanilla extract
¼ cup semisweet chocolate chips
3 tablespoons halved dried cherries

Position a rack in the center of the oven and preheat the oven to 350°F. Line three cups of a jumbo muffin pan (¾-cup capacity) with paper liners, or lightly butter the bottoms (only) of the cups and rub a little butter around the rim of each cup. (This will help them to form a rounded top.) Set the muffin pan aside.

Place the flour, baking powder, baking soda, salt, and nutmeg in a medium bowl; whisk to blend. Mix in half of the granola. Make a well in the center of the mixture.

Place the buttermilk, brown sugar, egg, oil, and vanilla in a bowl; whisk to blend well. Pour into the center of the flour mixture; stir just until the dry ingredients are moistened. Stir in the chocolate chips and dried cherries just until combined. Spoon the batter into the prepared muffin cups, dividing it evenly among them. Spoon the remaining granola over the muffin batter, and press it in lightly to adhere. Fill the empty muffin cups halfway with water to prevent them from scorching. Bake the muffins until a toothpick inserted into the center of one comes out clean, 23 to 25 minutes.

Remove the muffin pan from the oven and place it on a wire rack to cool for 5 minutes. Carefully pour the water out of the empty muffin cups. Turn the muffins out of the cups and let them cool, upright, on the wire rack for at least 10 minutes before serving. Serve warm or at room temperature. (These are best eaten the day they are baked but will keep up to 1 day in a plastic bag at room temperature.)

Note: To make regular-size muffins, line five standard muffin cups with paper liners or butter the cups as directed above. Spoon the batter into the cups and bake as directed, 15 to 18 minutes.

Makes 3 jumbo-size muffins or 5 regular-size muffins

෨෧

Java Choco-Banana Muffins

When my oldest daughter was in elementary school, I read a newspaper article to her that touted bananas as the perfect food to eat for breakfast before a test; they purportedly increase your memory power. I do not know if it was true or not, but the girl ate one every test day thereafter and she sailed all the way through high school with honors.

At the beginning of her own journey, my third-grade daughter is quite fond of this fruit and I am sure she will listen to her sister's scholarly advice. She loves them so much that these moist, rich-tasting muffins are a frequent request.

For the topping
2 tablespoons all-purpose flour
1 tablespoon firmly packed light brown sugar
Pinch of ground cinnamon
1 tablespoon unsalted butter
2 tablespoons chopped walnuts
2 tablespoons milk or semisweet chocolate chips

For the muffin batter
½ cup sliced banana (about ½ large banana)
3 tablespoons unsalted butter, at room temperature
¼ cup firmly packed light brown sugar
2 tablespoons granulated sugar
2 tablespoons well-beaten egg
½ teaspoon instant dark coffee or espresso powder

½ teaspoon pure vanilla extract

¼ teaspoon baking powder

⅛ teaspoon baking soda

⅛ teaspoon salt

½ cup plus 2 tablespoons all-purpose flour

⅓ cup milk or semisweet chocolate chips

Position a rack in the center of the oven and preheat the oven to 350°F. Line three cups of a jumbo muffin pan (¾-cup capacity) with paper liners, or lightly butter the bottoms (only) of the cups and rub a little butter around the rim of each cup. (This will help them to form a rounded top.) Set the muffin pan aside.

Make the topping: Place the flour, brown sugar, and cinnamon in a small bowl. Mix in the butter with your fingers or a fork until crumbly. Mix in the walnuts and chocolate chips and set aside.

Make the muffin batter: Place the banana, butter, brown sugar, granulated sugar, egg, coffee powder, vanilla, baking powder, baking soda, and salt in a food processor fitted with the knife blade. Process until smooth and blended, about 15 seconds, stopping once to scrape down the sides of the bowl. Add the flour and pulse just until blended, about 6 pulses. Scrape down the sides of the bowl and add the chocolate chips; pulse until mixed into the batter, about three times. Spoon the batter into the prepared muffin cups, dividing it evenly among them. (They will be filled about half-full.) Sprinkle with the topping. Fill the empty muffin cups halfway with water to prevent them from scorching. Bake the muffins until a toothpick inserted into the center of one comes out clean, 23 to 27 minutes.

Remove the muffin pan from the oven and place it on a wire rack to cool for 5 minutes. Carefully pour the water out of the empty muffin cups. Turn the muffins out of the cups and let them cool, upright, on the wire rack for at least

10 minutes before serving. Serve warm or at room temperature. (These are best eaten the day they are baked but will keep up to 1 day in a plastic bag at room temperature.)

Note: To make regular-size muffins, line five standard muffin cups with paper liners or butter the cups as directed above. Spoon the batter into the cups and bake as directed, 15 to 18 minutes.

Makes 3 jumbo-size muffins or 5 regular-size muffins

∾

Oatmeal Chocolate Chip Scones

Several years ago, a friend of mine finally released the secret to his dense chocolate chip cookies. He substituted ground oats for some of the flour. I figured that would be a good idea for chocolate chip scones, and boy, was I right. These are tender, sweet, and flaky, and full of chocolate chips. To go with them, you will want a big mug of coffee, the newspaper or a good book, and a comfy place to chill and nibble.

2 tablespoons cold, unsalted butter
¼ cup plus 2 tablespoons old-fashioned oats, uncooked
¼ cup plus 2 tablespoons all-purpose flour
1 tablespoon plus ½ teaspoon sugar, divided
½ teaspoon baking powder
⅛ teaspoon salt
⅓ cup semisweet chocolate chips or chunks
1 tablespoon half-and-half
1 tablespoon well-beaten egg

Position a rack in the center of the oven and preheat the oven to 375°F. Line a baking sheet with parchment paper and set it aside.

Cut the butter into ½-inch pieces; freeze while preparing other ingredients.

Place the oats in a food processor; process until finely ground, about 15 seconds. Add the flour, 1 tablespoon sugar, baking powder, and salt. Pulse until well combined, 3 to 4 pulses. Sprinkle the butter pieces over the flour mixture;

pulse until butter pieces are no larger than peas, about 7 pulses. Add chocolate chips, half-and-half, and egg; cover and pulse until the dough is well combined and moist clumps form, about 7 pulses.

Transfer the dough to a work surface and form into a disk; divide the dough in half and gently form each half into a ball. Place the balls of dough on the prepared baking sheet, spacing them 2 inches apart. Press down lightly on the dough balls to make each of them 1 inch thick. Sprinkle the tops with the remaining ½ teaspoon sugar. Bake the scones until a toothpick inserted in the center of one comes out clean, 15 to 17 minutes.

Remove the baking sheet from the oven, and use a metal spatula to transfer the scones to a wire rack to cool. Serve warm or at room temperature. (These are best eaten the day they are baked.)

Makes 2 scones

ͻ·

Pumpkin Spice White Chocolate Scones

These scones will remind you of the flavor in a beloved fall pie, and they are even love-lier with white chocolate pieces throughout and forming a glaze for their tops. I also like to make mini versions of them: roll the dough into six balls, flatten them slightly, and bake them for 12 minutes, then drizzle them with the glaze.

2 tablespoons plus 1 teaspoon cold, unsalted butter

3 tablespoons canned pure pumpkin puree (not pumpkin pie filling)

1 tablespoon sour cream

1 tablespoon well-beaten egg

⅔ cup all-purpose flour

2 tablespoons sugar

¼ teaspoon baking powder

⅛ teaspoon baking soda

⅛ teaspoon salt

⅛ teaspoon ground ginger

⅛ teaspoon ground cinnamon

⅛ teaspoon freshly grated nutmeg

2 ounces fine-quality white chocolate, finely chopped, divided

1½ tablespoons heavy (whipping) cream

Use a piece of foil or waxed paper to hold the 2 tablespoons butter and grate it on the large holes of a handheld grater onto a wax paper–lined baking sheet. Freeze the butter until it is solid.

Position a rack in the center of the oven and preheat the oven to 375°F. Line a baking sheet with parchment paper and set it aside.

Place the pumpkin, sour cream, and egg in a small bowl and whisk to blend.

Place the flour, sugar, baking powder, baking soda, salt, and spices in a medium bowl. Whisk to blend. Add the frozen butter pieces and half of the chopped white chocolate, and toss. Add the pumpkin mixture, and stir with a fork just until a soft, rough dough forms. Knead with your hands in the bowl until it holds together.

Form the dough into three equal parts; roll into balls. Place the balls on the prepared baking sheet and pat each lightly into an even 1½-inch thickness. Bake the scones until they are dry to the touch, cracked, and a wooden pick inserted in the center of one comes out clean, about 18 minutes.

Remove the baking sheet from the oven, and use a spatula to transfer the scones to a wire rack to cool.

Place the cream and remaining 1 teaspoon butter in a microwave-safe bowl; microwave on high power until cream is simmering and the butter melts. Stir in the remaining half of the chopped white chocolate until smooth. Spoon over the scones. Serve warm or at room temperature. (These are best eaten the day they are baked.)

Makes 3 scones

ᦂ

Rich Sweet Vanilla Chocolate Chip Scones

For me, this is the ultimate scone. They are actually flaky; that is, you can see the layers baked in because the grated butter creates little pockets of steam and "lifts and separates" the dough as it bakes. So what you eat is tender, buttery, and flaky, with a crisp crust. Using half cake flour helps make the tender crumb, too.

Not too sweet, they are full of meltingly warm bits of chocolate and flakes of vanilla bean from the paste.

The butter will grate more efficiently if you freeze the 3-tablespoon portion until it is solid, about 15 to 20 minutes.

> 3 tablespoons cold, unsalted butter
> 1/2 tablespoon well-beaten egg
> 2 tablespoons buttermilk
> 1/2 teaspoon vanilla bean paste or pure vanilla extract
> 1/4 cup cake flour
> 1/4 cup all-purpose flour
> 2 tablespoons plus 1 teaspoon sugar, divided
> 1/8 teaspoon baking powder
> 1/8 teaspoon baking soda
> Pinch (1/16 teaspoon) salt
> 1/4 cup semisweet chocolate chips
> 1/2 tablespoon unsalted butter, melted

Grate the butter on the large holes of a handheld grater onto a wax paper–lined plate or baking sheet. Freeze the butter until it is solid, 15 to 20 minutes.

Position a rack in the center of the oven and preheat the oven to 425°F. Line a baking sheet with parchment paper and set it aside.

Place the egg, buttermilk, and vanilla bean paste in a small bowl; whisk to blend.

Place the flours, 2 tablespoons of the sugar, baking powder, baking soda, and salt in a medium bowl; whisk to blend. Working quickly, add the grated butter and chocolate chips to the flour mixture and toss to combine; add the egg mixture and stir just until the dry ingredients are moistened.

Turn the dough out onto the lined baking sheet. Flour your hands and knead the dough lightly 2 or 3 times, or until it holds together. Pat the dough out to form a 1-inch-thick disk. Score the disk into thirds using the tip of a sharp knife; brush the top with the melted butter and sprinkle with the remaining ½ teaspoon sugar.

Bake the scones until golden, 12 to 15 minutes. Remove the baking sheet from the oven, and use a spatula to transfer the scones to a wire rack to cool. Cut along the score marks into wedges. (These are best eaten the day they are baked.)

Makes 3 scones

ᕬᎧ

Cinnamon Chocolate Scones

This is the scone I know I can always make; I usually have all the ingredients on hand. If I find myself out of cream, milk works. The sweet cinnamon spice really defines the chocolate flavor without the need for much sugar, and these have great buttery scone texture. I like to eat them warm, dripping with the yummy glaze.

½ cup all-purpose flour
2 tablespoons sugar
2 tablespoons unsweetened cocoa powder
½ teaspoon ground cinnamon
⅛ teaspoon baking soda
⅛ teaspoon salt
2 tablespoons cold unsalted butter, diced
1 tablespoon well-beaten egg
2 tablespoons heavy (whipping) cream
½ teaspoon pure vanilla extract
Cinnamon Chocolate Glaze (recipe follows)

Position a rack in the center of the oven and preheat the oven to 375°F. Line a baking sheet with parchment paper and set it aside.

Place the flour, sugar, cocoa powder, cinnamon, baking soda, and salt in a food processor fitted with the knife blade. Process until blended. Add the butter pieces and pulse until the coarse crumbs form. Transfer the mixture to a medium bowl and make a well in the center.

Place the egg, cream, and vanilla in a small bowl and whisk to blend. Pour into the center of the dry ingredients; stir with a fork just until a soft dough holds together.

Form the dough into three equal parts; roll into balls. Place the balls on the prepared baking sheet and pat each lightly into an even 1-inch thickness. Sprinkle the remaining ½ teaspoon sugar evenly over the tops of the scones. Bake the scones until they are dry to the touch, cracked, and a wooden pick inserted in the center of one comes out clean, about 18 minutes.

Remove the baking sheet from the oven, and using a spatula, transfer the scones to a wire rack to cool. Spoon the Cinnamon Chocolate Glaze over scones, and serve warm or at room temperature. (They are best eaten the day they are baked.)

Makes 3 scones

Cinnamon Chocolate Glaze
3 tablespoons semisweet chocolate chips
2 teaspoons unsalted butter
2 teaspoons hot water
1 tablespoon confectioners' sugar
⅛ teaspoon ground cinnamon

Place the chocolate chips and butter in a small, microwave-safe bowl; microwave on medium power until soft, 30 to 45 seconds. Stir until smooth. Stir in hot water until blended; stir in confectioners' sugar and cinnamon.

Makes about 3 tablespoons

Banana Split Chocolate Chip Shortcakes

Double your chocolate pleasure with a chocolate chip shortcake, and serve it like a banana split, loaded with strawberries, bananas, and homemade chocolate and caramel sauces. Your inner child will love them!

For the shortcakes

½ cup all-purpose flour

2 tablespoons sugar

1 tablespoon unsweetened cocoa powder

¼ teaspoon baking powder

⅛ teaspoon baking soda

⅛ teaspoon salt

2 tablespoons cold, unsalted butter, diced

3 tablespoons semisweet chocolate chips

3 tablespoons cold whole milk

For the filling

¼ cup heavy (whipping) cream

1 tablespoon confectioners' sugar

For serving

Sliced fresh strawberries and bananas

Rich Caramel Sauce (recipe follows)

Homemade Chocolate Syrup (page 311)

Candied Pecans, optional (recipe follows)

Position a rack in the center of the oven and preheat the oven to 400°F. Line a baking sheet with parchment paper and set it aside.

Make the shortcakes: Place the flour, sugar, cocoa powder, baking powder, baking soda, and salt in a medium bowl and whisk to blend the dry ingredients. Cut in the butter until the lumps are no larger than small peas. Stir in the chocolate chips. Sprinkle 2 tablespoons of the milk over the crumb mixture and stir it lightly with a fork until the dough just holds together. Add the remaining tablespoon of milk if the dough is still dry and crumbly.

Divide the dough in half and gently form each half into a ball. Place the balls of dough on the prepared baking sheet, spacing them 2 inches apart. Press down lightly to make them 1 inch thick. Bake the shortcakes until a toothpick inserted in the center of one comes out clean, about 17 minutes. Remove the baking sheet from the oven and slide the parchment paper, with the shortcakes on it , onto a wire rack. Let cool for 15 minutes.

Make the filling: Place the cream and the confectioners' sugar in a small, deep mixing bowl and beat with a handheld electric mixer on high speed until firm peaks form.

To assemble the shortcakes, cut them in half horizontally. Place the bottom halves in shallow bowls and spoon the strawberries and bananas over the shortcake bottoms, dividing it evenly between them. Replace the shortcake tops. Drizzle the plate and the shortcakes with the Rich Caramel Sauce and the Homemade Chocolate Syrup. Sprinkle with the Candied Pecans if using. Serve immediately.

Makes 2 shortcakes

Rich Caramel Sauce
½ cup sugar
¼ cup plus 2 tablespoons heavy (whipping) cream

Combine the sugar and 2 tablespoons of water in a small saucepan over medium-high heat. Bring to a boil, stirring with a fork, and cook until the sugar dissolves, about 3 minutes. Reduce the heat to medium and cook, swirling the saucepan frequently, until the sugar syrup is golden amber in color, 7 to 9 minutes.

Remove the pan from the heat and gradually add the cream, stirring slowly and carefully; the caramel will sputter when the liquid is added. The sugar may seize and harden. If it does, return the pan to the heat and continue cooking until the sugar melts again, about 2 minutes. Serve the sauce immediately or store in a covered jar in the refrigerator for up to 1 week.

Makes ½ cup

Variation

Chocolate Coconut Shortcakes
To make this variation, add 2 tablespoons sweetened, flaked coconut to the flour mixture before cutting in the butter. To serve, sprinkle the shortcakes with toasted coconut instead of Candied Pecans.

Candied Pecans
½ cup chopped pecans
1½ teaspoons light corn syrup
1 tablespoon granulated sugar

Position a rack in the center of the oven. Preheat the oven to 325°F. Line a rimmed baking sheet with aluminum foil and set it aside.

Place the pecans and corn syrup in a small bowl and stir to mix. Add the sugar and toss to coat the pecans well. Working quickly so the sugar does not dissolve, spread the pecans on the baking sheet and bake until they are golden, 10 minutes. Remove the pecans from the oven. Stir to loosen the pecans from the foil; let them cool completely. Set the pecans aside. (The Candied Pecans can be made 1 day ahead; store them in an airtight container.)

Makes ½ cup

෭෨

Milk Chocolate Flake Shortcakes with Raspberries and Rich Milk Chocolate Caramel Sauce

A food processor turns these shortcakes into a one-bowl cinch to make; by pulsing in the diced chocolate, you finely flake it into the dough, giving the shortcake chocolate flecks of flavor throughout. Milk chocolate goes into the caramel sauce, too, giving it supremely rich body and extra-decadent taste. The dessert is very sweetly chocolate, a welcome sweet-tart, with a raspberry accent.

For the shortcakes

½ cup all-purpose flour

2 tablespoons plus 1 teaspoon sugar, divided

¼ teaspoon baking powder

¼ teaspoon baking soda

⅛ teaspoon salt

1 tablespoon cold unsalted butter, diced

1 ounce fine-quality milk chocolate, finely diced (¼-inch pieces)

2 tablespoons cold buttermilk

1 teaspoon well-beaten egg

For the filling

1½ cups fresh raspberries or strawberries

1 tablespoon sugar

1 tablespoon raspberry liqueur, such as Chambord or Framboise, optional

For serving
⅓ cup cold heavy (whipping) cream
1 tablespoon confectioners' sugar
Rich Milk Chocolate Caramel Sauce (recipe follows)

Position a rack in the center of the oven and preheat the oven to 400°F. Line a baking sheet with parchment paper and set it aside.

Make the shortcakes: Place the flour, 2 tablespoons of the sugar, baking powder, baking soda, and salt in a food processor bowl fitted with the knife blade; process to blend the dry ingredients, 2 to 3 seconds. Sprinkle the butter pieces over the flour mixture and pulse until the butter pieces are no larger than small peas, about 7 pulses. Sprinkle the chocolate over the mixture, and pulse until combined, 3 to 4 pulses. Sprinkle the buttermilk and egg over the mixture and pulse just until moist clumps form, about 7 pulses. (Add 1 more tablespoon buttermilk, if dough is too dry.)

Transfer the dough to a work surface and form into a disk; divide the dough in half and gently form each half into a ball. Place the balls of dough on the prepared baking sheet spacing 2 inches apart. Press down lightly to make each of them 1 inch thick. Sprinkle the tops with the remaining teaspoon sugar. Bake the shortcakes until a toothpick inserted in the center of one comes out clean, 15 to 17 minutes. Remove the baking sheet from the oven and slide the parchment paper, with the shortcakes on it, onto a wire rack to cool for 15 minutes.

Make the fruit filling: While the shortcakes are cooling, place ¼ cup of the raspberries, sugar, and liqueur, if using, in a small bowl, and mash the berries. Stir in the whole raspberries.

Place the cream and the confectioners' sugar in a small, deep mixing bowl and beat with a handheld electric mixer on high speed until firm peaks form.

To assemble the shortcakes, carefully cut them in half horizontally. Place the bottom halves in shallow bowls and spoon the raspberries and juices on the bottoms, dividing it evenly between them. Top with the whipped cream; replace the shortcake tops. Drizzle the plate and the shortcakes with the Rich Milk Chocolate Caramel Sauce. Serve immediately.

Makes 2 shortcakes

Rich Milk Chocolate Caramel Sauce
½ cup heavy (whipping) cream
½ cup firmly packed light brown sugar
1 cinnamon stick (1½ inches long)
2 tablespoons canned, sweetened condensed milk
2 ounces fine-quality milk chocolate, chopped

Place the cream, brown sugar, and cinnamon stick in a small, heavy saucepan over medium heat and bring to a boil, stirring constantly until the sugar dissolves. Continue to boil, stirring occasionally, until the mixture reduces to ½ cup, about 5 minutes. Remove the cinnamon stick and stir in the condensed milk and chocolate until smooth. Serve warm or at room temperature. Store any leftovers in a covered container in the refrigerator.

Makes about ⅔ cup

Better with Chocolate

∽

There are some things that cannot help but taste better with chocolate in them. For instance, I did not exactly jump for joy when my mother announced that she had baked date nut bread. But when my sister and I concocted the idea of putting chocolate in her bread, it changed everything—and now we all love it.

Then I played around with homemade sweet rolls and found that chocolate in the filling just made them all that much more enticing. If that works, what would chocolate do to baklava? It was divine in the nut filling.

Moving on to cookies that normally do not contain chocolate, I tried it in graham crackers and then gingersnaps. Why not? They both were decidedly better with chocolate.

With the sky the limit, I put chocolate into some more breads, pies, and puddings that are not known for their chocolate properties. Some made the cut, others came out of the oven, forced and unrealistic with chocolate in them—like lemon squares or coconut pie.

I guarantee you will think that the winners in this chapter are better with chocolate, too!

ALL ABOUT CHOCOLATE VARIETIES

from the cacao bean comes all things chocolate—chocolate liquor, cocoa butter, and cocoa powder. Cacao pods are fermented and then roasted and ground into a fine paste that can be separated into two components: cacao solids (commonly called cocoa powder) and cocoa butter. Each chocolate maker, called a *chocolatier*, combines these in different proportions. In general, the chocolatier will combine the cocoa solids, cocoa butter, and sugar with other ingredients—emulsifiers, flavors, and milk solids if making milk chocolate—and forms his mixture into blocks and bars of chocolate.

The cacao content marked on the package will indicate how sweet the chocolate will taste. For example, "60 percent Cacao" on a label tells that the chocolate consists of 60 percent cocoa butter and chocolate liquor, in any combination, and the remaining 40 percent is made up of sugar and those optional ingredients. Bars labeled with a higher percentage of cacao will taste more intensely chocolate and less sweet. Finding the right chocolate is a matter of tasting and finding the balance you like.

The quality of the chocolate does not relate to the percentage of cacao, by the way, but rather the quality of the origin of the chocolate. Behind good-quality chocolate bars, there is a huge investment of time and money and effort to find the beans and produce the chocolate. To distinguish quality, smell it. If it is of poor quality, you will immediately smell sugar and artificial vanilla or metallic nuances. Tasting it will confirm what you smell. If the chocolate is of high quality, the smell and taste will be more complex; nothing like sugar or vanilla will scream at your senses. The nuances of taste and smell will be complex and of the land—earthy, fruity, flowery, exactly the same as wine.

What Gives Chocolate its Distinctive "Melt-in-the-Mouth" Feel?

Chocolate liquor and cocoa powder give chocolate its taste, but the cocoa butter gives it that matchless texture. It is a naturally occurring vegetable fat that is solid at room temperature but melts when it comes in contact with your body temperature. As a matter of fact, chocolatiers pride themselves on how their chocolate melts in your mouth; the chocolate is crafted for you to savor as it melts smoothly and slowly.

Chocolate Baklava

When I developed the Baklava recipe for *Small-Batch Baking,* I was proud. Even some Greek cooks, who have baked baklava since they were old enough to help their yayas roll out homemade phyllo, loved the small-batch version. I cannot resist a piece of the soaked phyllo and sweet nut layers, often flavored with honey, orange, and a variety of nuts.

But when this came out of the pan just right, I knew I could never eat another piece of baklava without longing for this one with chocolate. I expected the chocolate to ooze out of the pastry layers and the combined nut and chocolate layers not to soak up the syrup well, but I completely misjudged. The cold syrup poured over the hot layers "shocked" and set the melted chocolate, which blended into the nut layer more decadently than I could have imagined.

You will have to give it a try to see how beautifully this recipe works.

For the syrup
⅓ cup sugar
⅓ cup honey
½ teaspoon pure vanilla extract
½ teaspoon almond extract
1 or 2 tablespoons Amaretto or Frangelico

For the pastry
½ cup slivered almonds or toasted, skinned hazelnuts, chopped
2 ounces bittersweet chocolate, coarsely chopped
2 tablespoons sugar

½ teaspoon ground cinnamon

7 sheets frozen phyllo dough, thawed

5 tablespoons unsalted butter, melted

Make the syrup: Place the sugar, honey, and ⅓ cup water in a small saucepan. Bring to a boil over medium-high heat, stirring constantly until the sugar melts. Continue boiling 1 minute without stirring. Remove the pan from the heat and let the syrup stand at room temperature until it is cool. Stir in the vanilla, almond extract, and liqueur, and pour the syrup into a glass jar or measuring cup. Cover and refrigerate the syrup until it is cold, about 2 hours.

Make the pastry: Position a rack in the center of the oven and preheat the oven to 325°F. Line a 9 × 5-inch loaf pan with a large piece of aluminum foil, carefully pressing the foil into the corners and up the sides of the loaf pan and extending the edges of the foil 1½ inches above the loaf pan. Fold the edges of the foil down the outside of the pan. Set the pan aside.

Place the nuts, chocolate, and sugar in a food processor bowl. Pulse the mixture until nuts and chocolate are finely chopped and are about the same size, 30 to 35 pulses. Transfer to a bowl and stir in the cinnamon.

Stack the sheets of phyllo on a work surface and cut them in half crosswise, making fourteen half-sheets. Stack the two halves together. While you are working with the phyllo, to keep it from drying out, keep the stack of phyllo sheets covered with a damp, clean kitchen towel.

Working with one sheet of phyllo at a time and starting with a lengthwise edge, fold over 2 inches and fit it into the bottom of the prepared loaf pan. Brush it lightly with melted butter. Repeat the folding with four more sheets, brushing the top of each folded sheet with butter. Sprinkle half of the nut mixture over the top sheet. Add another folded sheet of phyllo and brush it with butter; repeat with three more folded sheets, brushing the top of each folded sheet with butter. Sprinkle the remaining nut mixture over this top sheet. Add five more folded sheets, brushing the top of each one with butter.

Using a sharp knife, make three cuts across the width of the phyllo, cutting through just the top layers and spacing the cuts evenly. Make one cut down the length of the phyllo, resulting in rectangular shapes. (If you wish, cut each rectangle into odd-shaped triangles.) Bake the baklava until it is golden brown, about 30 minutes.

Drizzle the cold syrup over the hot baklava. Using a sharp knife, deepen the earlier cut lines to reach all the way through the layers. Cover the baklava and let it stand at room temperature for the syrup to soak through the layers, about 4 hours.

To serve, use the foil to help you lift the baklava from the loaf pan and place it on a work surface. Using a thin metal spatula, lift the pieces onto a serving platter or individual plates. Pour the accumulated syrup over the pieces of baklava. (The baklava can be made 2 days in advance. Bring it to room temperature, which takes about 2 hours; then remove it from the pan.)

Makes 8 pieces

Chocolate Chèvre Cheesecakes

Goat cheese imparts a fresh tangy taste to the filling, and it is lovely with the bittersweet chocolate and kiss of honey. To make sure it is creamy smooth, the ingredients are processed in a blender. Along with the pistachio crust, these are sophisticated in flavor.

¼ cup roasted salted pistachios, very finely chopped
2 tablespoons all-purpose flour
1 tablespoon sugar
1½ tablespoons unsalted butter, melted
3 ounces fine-quality bittersweet chocolate, divided, chopped
1 teaspoon unsalted butter
4 ounces mild fresh chèvre (goat cheese), at room temperature
3 ounces cream cheese, at room temperature
¼ cup honey
1 large egg
1 teaspoon pure vanilla extract
3 tablespoons sour cream
Chopped roasted pistachios for garnish

Place a rack in the center of the oven and preheat the oven to 325°F. Lightly butter the insides of two 8-ounce cans (see page 8). Place the cans on a piece of parchment paper and trace around the circumference. Cut out two parchment rounds and line the bottoms of each can with them. Cut out two 11 × 2-inch strips of parchment paper, and use them to line the insides of cans; the parchment paper should reach the top of the cans. Place the cans in an 8- or 9-inch square baking pan and set the pan aside.

Place the chopped pistachios, flour, and sugar in a bowl; stir to mix well. Stir in the melted butter until the mixture is moistened. Spoon the nut mixture into the prepared cans, dividing it evenly. Gently press the crumb mixture down with your fingertips. Bake until the color of the crust begins to darken, 8 to 10 minutes.

Remove the baking pan from the oven and transfer it, with the cans, onto a wire rack. Let cool. Keep the oven on.

Place 2½ ounces of the chocolate and the 1 teaspoon butter in a microwave-safe bowl; microwave on medium power until soft, about 2 minutes. Stir until it is smooth. Let it cool.

Place the chèvre, cream cheese, honey, egg, and vanilla in a blender container. Process until the mixture is smooth and creamy, 20 to 30 seconds, scraping down the blender container as necessary. Add the melted chocolate mixture, and process until smooth. Pour the batter on top of the pistachio crusts, dividing it evenly between the cans. Scrape the batter that clings to the side of the blender container into the cans.

Pour boiling water into the baking pan to come halfway up the sides of the cans. Bake until the cheesecakes are just set, about 28 to 30 minutes.

Meanwhile, place the remaining ½ ounce chocolate in a microwave-safe bowl; microwave until soft, about 30 seconds. Stir until the chocolate is smooth. Stir in the sour cream. When the cheesecakes are just set, remove the baking pan from the oven. Spoon the sour cream mixture gently over the tops of the cheesecakes; return the cheesecakes to the oven and continue baking 2 minutes more. Remove the pan from the oven and transfer the cans to a wire rack, and let cool completely. Cover and refrigerate the cheesecakes 6 hours or overnight.

To serve, run a sharp knife around the sides of the cans to loosen the cheesecakes. Turn the cakes out, remove the parchment paper, and place them upright on serving plates. Garnish with chopped roasted pistachios. The cheesecakes will keep, covered, in the refrigerator for 1 week.

Makes 2 cheesecakes

༄

Warm Chocolate Chess Pies

This one shows my Southern roots. There are two things we Southern cooks know how to use in our breads, cakes, and pies: cornmeal and buttermilk. Chess pies are egg custard pies that use cornmeal for thickening rather than flour. The tang of buttermilk is barely noticeable in these pies, but it is responsible for the richness of the custard.

2 partially-baked Rich Sweet Pastry shells (page 122), baked in 4 × 1⅜-inch
    tart pans with removable bottoms, still in the pans
2 ounces fine-quality bittersweet or semisweet chocolate, chopped
¼ cup buttermilk (not nonfat)
3 tablespoons well-beaten egg
2 tablespoons sugar
2 teaspoons cornmeal
½ teaspoon pure vanilla extract
Pinch of salt

Position a rack in the center of the oven and preheat the oven to 350°F. Put the tart pans on a baking sheet for easier handling and set it aside.

Place the chocolate in a small, microwave-safe bowl; microwave at medium power or until soft, about 1 minute. Stir until smooth. Set aside.

Place the buttermilk, egg, sugar, cornmeal, vanilla, and salt in a small, deep bowl; stir well. Whisk in the chocolate mixture until blended. Pour the filling into the tart crusts, dividing it evenly between them.

Bake the tarts until the filling is set in the center, about 25 minutes. Remove the baking sheet from the oven and transfer the tarts to a wire rack to cool for 15 minutes. Then carefully remove the tarts from the pans and place them on serving plates. Serve the tarts warm with ice cream or whipped cream.

Makes 2 tarts

Bittersweet Caramel Nut Tarts

Everywhere I went on tour for the first *Small-Batch Baking* book, I prepared the non-chocolate version of this recipe from that book because it was so doggone delicious. But I always wondered *what if*? *What if* the tarts were just a little more over the top, say, with chocolate in them? Here was my chance to push it, and my instincts were right.

Now this version is my all-time favorite Christmas dessert. Several years ago, my ninety-five-year-old Aunt Cora gave me a set of antique, gold-rimmed dishes, and they are what I pull out of the china cabinet to serve these beautiful tarts on.

> 2 partially baked Basic Pastry shells (page 118), baked in 4½ × ¾-inch tart
>   pans with removable bottoms, still in the pans
> 2½ ounces fine-quality bittersweet chocolate, divided, finely chopped
> ¼ cup pecan halves
> ¼ cup walnut halves
> ¼ cup blanched almonds
> 2 tablespoons unsalted butter
> ¼ cup plus 2 tablespoons firmly packed light brown sugar
> 2 tablespoons heavy (whipped) cream

Position a rack in the center of the oven and preheat the oven to 350°F. Place the tart pans on a baking sheet for easier handling and set it aside. Sprinkle 1½ ounces of the chopped chocolate evenly over the bottoms of the pastry shells. Place the baking sheet in the oven until the chocolate is soft, about 2 minutes; spread on the bottoms of the pastry shells and let them cool completely.

Coarsely chop the nuts.

Place the butter and brown sugar in a small, heavy saucepan and bring to a simmer over medium heat, stirring constantly. Simmer 1 minute. Stir in the cream; stir in the nuts. Pour the mixture over the chocolate in the pastry shells, dividing it evenly. Bake the tarts until the filling is bubbling and is a few shades darker, about 15 minutes.

Remove the baking sheet from the oven, transfer the tart pans to a wire rack, and let them cool completely.

Place the remaining 1 ounce of chopped chocolate in a microwave-safe bowl; microwave on high power until soft, about 1 minute. Stir until smooth. Dip the tines of a fork into the melted chocolate and drizzle it attractively over the tarts. Let the tarts stand at room temperature until the chocolate sets. Remove the tarts from the pans and serve. (The tarts can be prepared 1 day ahead; cover and store at room temperature.)

Makes 2 tarts

Chocolate Gingersnaps

If you ask me, these are anytime cookies. I love them with goat cheese on the top, like a canapé, with tea in the afternoon. I adore them with my morning latte to spice up the morning. And for dessert, I like to curl up on the couch and dip the cookies into a small dish of just chocolate ice cream.

You can eat these right out of the oven; when they are warm, they are chewy, and they firm up as they chill. They are perfect for the ice cream sandwich variation following; the cookies will stay crispy after they are frozen with the ice cream between them.

3 tablespoons granulated sugar

2 tablespoons unsalted butter, softened

1 tablespoon unsulfered molasses

1½ teaspoons beaten egg yolk

¼ cup plus 1 tablespoon all-purpose flour

1½ tablespoons unsweetened cocoa powder

⅛ teaspoon baking soda

⅛ teaspoon salt

½ teaspoon ground ginger

⅛ teaspoon ground allspice

1½ to 2 tablespoons sanding sugar for sprinkling, optional

Position a rack in the center of the oven and preheat the oven to 350°F. Line a baking sheet with parchment paper and set aside.

Place the sugar, butter, molasses, and egg yolk in a small, deep mixing bowl. Beat on low speed of a handheld electric mixer until blended, about 20 seconds. Increase the speed to medium and beat until the mixture is well blended, about 30 seconds.

Place the flour, cocoa powder, baking soda, salt, and spices in a small bowl. Stir with a whisk to blend. Beat into the butter mixture.

Roll the dough into six equal-size balls, spacing them 2 inches apart on the prepared baking sheet. Flatten the balls with the bottom of a drinking glass buttered and dipped in sugar. Sprinkle the tops of the cookies with sanding sugar, if desired. Bake the cookies until dry on the top, 10 to 11 minutes. Slide the parchment paper with the cookies on it onto a wire rack and then let them cool completely. Use a metal spatula to lift the cookies from the paper.

Makes 6 cookies

Variation

Chocolate Gingersnap Ice Cream Sandwiches Scoop ½ cup slightly softened, chocolate ice cream or sorbet on three cookies and top with the three remaining cookies. Wrap the sandwiches individually in aluminum foil and freeze until firm.

Makes 3 ice cream sandwiches

Chocolate Graham Crackers

My girls are big fans of chocolate graham crackers; they eat them straight with a tall glass of cold milk, and they love them with peanut butter and sliced bananas sandwiched between two squares for breakfast and snacks. As for me, they are a terrific dunking cookie with a soy latte.

But all of us love this homemade version the best; the graham flour gives them extra texture and I know how healthy the flour is, with its extra helping of wheat bran.

I find graham flour at organic food markets in my area, but it is not always readily available. Whole wheat flour is a good substitute but it will not quite give you the same characteristic crunch. To get that crushed nut texture, you would have to mix all-purpose flour with wheat bran and wheat germ in perfect proportions to stand in for graham flour.

But even whole wheat flour gives these cookies wonderful texture, and in my opinion, it is the chocolate that trumps all, anyway!

    ¼ cup plus 1½ tablespoons all-purpose flour
    ¼ cup graham flour
    1½ tablespoons unsweetened cocoa powder
    Pinch of baking soda
    ⅛ teaspoon salt
    2½ tablespoons unsalted butter, softened
    2 tablespoons firmly packed brown sugar

1 tablespoon honey
1 tablespoon well-beaten egg
¼ teaspoon vanilla extract
1 tablespoon sugar

Place the flours, cocoa powder, baking soda, and salt in a small bowl and whisk to blend well.

Place the butter, brown sugar, honey, egg, and vanilla in a small, deep mixing bowl; beat on high speed using a handheld electric mixer until the mixture is well blended, about 20 seconds. Beat in the flour mixture to make a firm dough. Transfer the dough to a piece of plastic wrap, flatten it into a disk, and wrap it well; refrigerate until it is firm enough to roll, about 30 minutes.

Position a rack in the center of the oven and preheat the oven to 350°F. Line a baking sheet with parchment paper and set it aside.

Roll out the dough on a floured surface into a rough square that is ¼ inch thick. Cut the dough into 3-inch squares; and place on the prepared baking sheet, spacing them 1 inch apart. Reroll scraps and cut into squares; transfer to the baking sheet. Sprinkle the dough evenly with the sugar. If desired, score the tops of the graham crackers with the tip of a sharp knife and the tines of a fork to make them look like the store-bought version.

Bake the cookies until the edges are beginning to brown, 8 to 10 minutes; they will harden as they cool. Slide the parchment paper, with the cookies, onto a wire rack and let them cool completely. Use a metal spatula to lift the cookies from the paper.

Makes 5 cookies

Variations

Hazelnut Milk Chocolate–Covered Graham Crackers: When cookies are cool, place 2 tablespoons Nutella (chocolate-hazelnut spread) and ¼ cup milk chocolate chips in a small, microwave-safe bowl. Microwave on medium power until soft, about 1 to 1½ minutes; stir until smooth. Spoon and spread on the tops of cookies. Refrigerate until the chocolate hardens, about 30 minutes.

Makes 5 cookies

෨

Chocolate Biscuit Rolls

If it can be baked, it can have chocolate in it. That is the way I felt about the small-batch cinnamon rolls I make for breakfast if the morning is leisurely. Just a little chopped chocolate rolled up in the biscuit dough makes them taste incredible.

> 1 tablespoon unsalted butter, melted
> ½ cup all-purpose flour
> 2 tablespoons sugar, divided
> ½ teaspoon baking powder
> ¼ teaspoon baking soda
> ⅛ teaspoon salt
> 1 tablespoon plus 2 teaspoons cold, unsalted butter, cut into small bits, and frozen
> 2 tablespoons cold buttermilk
> ¼ teaspoon ground cinnamon
> 1 ounce bittersweet or semisweet chocolate, coarsely chopped

Position a rack in the center of the oven and preheat the oven to 375°F. Line the bottom of an 8 × 4-inch loaf pan lengthwise and up the short ends with a piece of parchment paper. Brush the paper and up the sides of the pan with half of the melted butter. Set the pan aside.

Place the flour, 1 tablespoon of the sugar, the baking powder, baking soda, and salt in a small bowl. Whisk to blend. Sprinkle the butter pieces over the flour mixture; cut them into the flour mixture using a pastry blender until the lumps of butter are no larger than small peas. Sprinkle the buttermilk over the mixture and toss lightly with a fork just until the dough begins to hold together, just a few seconds. If necessary, sprinkle additional buttermilk, by teaspoonfuls, over the dough and mix in to make a soft dough.

Flour your hands and lightly knead the dough in the bowl five times. Sprinkle a teaspoon or two of flour on a piece of wax paper or on a cutting board and put the dough in the center. Pat the dough out to form a 5 × 3½ × ½-inch rectangle.

Place the remaining 1 tablespoon sugar and cinnamon in a small bowl and stir well. Sprinkle half of the mixture over the top of the dough. Sprinkle the chopped chocolate evenly over the dough. Roll up the dough tightly, beginning with the short end, pushing any stray falling chocolate back into the rolls. Cut the roll into three equal-size pieces and arrange them, cut sides down, in the loaf pan.

Brush the remaining melted butter over the tops of the biscuits and sprinkle with the remaining half of the cinnamon sugar. Bake until the biscuits are puffed and golden, 14 to 15 minutes. Serve warm or at room temperature.

Makes 3 biscuits

Chocolate Carrot Cake Muffins

What a difference chocolate makes! These muffins could be served as cake, because they are rich with carrot cake ingredients and have a luscious cream cheese glaze. They are definitely a treat, but they have healthy stuff in them, too.

When you drain the pineapple to use in the batter, make sure you save some of the juice for making the glaze.

> ½ cup plus 1 tablespoon all-purpose flour
> 3 tablespoons sugar
> ¼ teaspoon baking powder
> ⅛ teaspoon baking soda
> ¼ teaspoon salt
> ¼ teaspoon ground cinnamon
> 1½ ounces bittersweet or semisweet chocolate, finely chopped
> 2 tablespoons vegetable oil
> 2 tablespoons well-beaten egg
> ½ teaspoon pure vanilla extract
> ⅓ cup grated carrots
> 3 tablespoons well-drained canned crushed pineapple, 2 teaspoons of the juice reserved
> 3 tablespoons chopped walnuts
> 2 tablespoons raisins
> Cream Cheese Glaze (recipe follows)
> Toasted coconut, optional

Position a rack in the center of the oven and preheat the oven to 350°F. Line three cups of a jumbo muffin pan (¾-cup capacity) with paper liners, or lightly butter the bottoms (only) of the cups and rub a little butter around the rim of each cup. (This will help them to form a rounded top.) Set the muffin pan aside.

Place the flour, sugar, baking powder, baking soda, salt, and cinnamon in a food processor bowl; pulse to mix the ingredients, 2 to 3 pulses. Sprinkle the chocolate over the mixture and process until the chocolate is very finely chopped, about 10 seconds. Transfer the mixture to a bowl; make a well in the center of the mixture.

Place the oil, egg, and vanilla in a bowl; stir well. Mix in the carrots, pineapple, walnuts, and raisins. Pour into the center of the flour mixture, and stir lightly just until the dry ingredients are moistened. Spoon the batter into the prepared muffin cups, dividing it evenly between them. Fill the empty muffin cups halfway with water to prevent them from scorching. Bake the muffins until a toothpick inserted into the center of one comes out clean, about 25 minutes.

Remove the muffin pan from the oven and place it on a wire rack to cool for 5 minutes. Carefully pour the water out of the empty muffin cups. Turn the muffins out of the cups and let them cool completely on the rack. Drizzle the tops of the muffins with Cream Cheese Glaze. Sprinkle with toasted coconut, if desired. (These are best eaten the day they are baked but will keep up to 1 day in a plastic bag at room temperature.)

Makes 3 muffins

Cream Cheese Glaze
1 ounce cream cheese, at room temperature
½ cup confectioners' sugar, sifted
2 teaspoons reserved pineapple juice

Place all of the ingredients in a bowl and whisk together until the glaze is smooth and creamy.

Makes ¼ cup

Variations

Spiced Chocolate Zucchini Muffins: Grated zucchini are also a great vegetable to add to muffins. Add the pineapple, walnuts, and raisins to the batter as the recipe calls for, or you can omit all of those and stir ½ cup grated zucchini into the batter instead. Bake them as the recipe directs.

Chocolate Apple Walnut Muffins: These are so wonderful on a fall morning. Substitute apple pie spice for the cinnamon and ½ cup grated peeled apple for the carrots in the batter, omitting the pineapple. Omit the raisins and stir in ¼ cup chopped walnuts. Bake them as the recipe directs.

ᑐᑐ

Morning Glory Muffins

These muffins are so full of yummy things that you cannot put your finger on what it is that makes you love them. In my opinion, it is the grated chocolate that adds subtle depth of flavor; apple and coconut gives them layers of sweetness, not just a charge of sugar. The grated zucchini adds moisture that keeps them from drying out, even if you eat one the next day. I like to measure the dry ingredients, grate the chocolate, and prep the zucchini and pecans the night before, then grate the apple and complete the recipe for baking the next morning.

For extra fiber and vitamins, substitute ¼ cup whole wheat flour for ¼ cup of the all-purpose flour.

> ½ cup plus 1 tablespoon all-purpose flour
> ¼ teaspoon baking powder
> ¼ teaspoon baking soda
> ⅛ teaspoon salt
> ½ teaspoon ground cinnamon
> 1 ounce semisweet chocolate, grated on large holes of handheld grater
> ¼ cup sugar
> 3 tablespoons well-beaten egg
> 3 tablespoons vegetable oil
> ½ teaspoon pure vanilla extract
> ½ cup grated zucchini
> 2 tablespoons grated apple
> 3 tablespoons chopped pecans

2 tablespoons raisins

2 tablespoons packed sweetened flaked coconut

Position a rack in the center of the oven and preheat the oven to 350°F. Line three cups of a jumbo muffin pan (¾-cup capacity) with paper liners, or lightly butter the bottoms (only) of the cups and rub a little butter around the rim of each cup. (This will help them to form a rounded top.) Set the muffin pan aside.

Place the flour, baking powder, baking soda, salt, and cinnamon in a medium bowl, and whisk to blend the dry ingredients. Sprinkle the grated chocolate over the mixture and toss with a fork until the chocolate is evenly distributed. Make a well in the center of the mixture.

Place the sugar, egg, oil, and vanilla in a bowl; stir well. Mix in the zucchini and apple. Pour into the center of the flour mixture, and stir lightly just until dry ingredients are moistened. Fold in the pecans, raisins, and coconut. Spoon into the prepared muffin cups. Fill the empty muffin cups halfway with water to prevent them from scorching.

Bake the muffins until a toothpick inserted into the center of one comes out clean, about 25 minutes.

Remove the muffin pan from the oven and place it on a wire rack to cool for 5 minutes. Carefully pour the water out of the empty muffin cups. Turn the muffins out of the cups and let them cool, upright, on the wire rack for at least 10 minutes before serving. Serve warm or at room temperature. (These are best eaten the day they are baked but will keep up to 1 day in a plastic bag at room temperature.)

Note: To make regular-size muffins, line five standard muffin cups with paper liners or butter the cups as directed above. Spoon the batter into the cups and bake as directed, 15 to 18 minutes.

Makes 3 jumbo-size muffins or 5 regular-size muffins

Chocolate Chip Date Nut "Breads"

My mother and her two sisters made date nut bread in Maxwell House coffee cans in the 1950s and well after that. Just as casseroles had their heyday in the '50s and '60s with the emergence of convenience products, it was hip to recycle one-pound coffee cans into baking vessels for date nut bread.

Recycling cans for baking seemed like a good idea to me, but my date nut breads needed a little more decadence. Since, in my house, it is not sweet if it does not contain chocolate, this date nut bread got a chocolate chip update.

> Softened butter for greasing the cans
> ⅓ cup pitted chopped dates
> 3 tablespoons whole milk
> 3 tablespoons vegetable oil
> 1½ tablespoons well-beaten egg
> ¼ cup plus 3 tablespoons all-purpose flour
> ⅓ cup firmly packed light brown sugar
> 2 tablespoons unsweetened cocoa powder
> ¼ teaspoon baking soda
> ⅛ teaspoon salt
> ¼ cup semisweet chocolate chips
> ¼ cup chopped walnuts or pecans

Place a rack in the center of the oven and preheat to 325°F. Lightly butter the insides of two 14.5-ounce cans (see page 8 for preparing cans). Line the bottoms of the cans with rounds of parchment paper. Place on a baking sheet for easier handling and set aside.

Chop dates even more finely, into about ⅛-inch pieces. Place the milk and dates in a small, microwave-safe bowl; microwave on high power until hot, 45 seconds. Let the dates and milk cool to room temperature, stirring occasionally and pressing the dates occasionally to submerge in the milk. Stir in the oil and beaten egg.

Place the flour, brown sugar, cocoa powder, baking soda, and salt in a medium bowl. Stir to mix the dry ingredients well. Add the date mixture; stir just until the dry ingredients are moistened. Stir in the chocolate chips and walnuts.

Scrape the batter into the prepared cans, dividing it evenly. Bake the cakes until a toothpick inserted in the centers comes out clean, 33 to 35 minutes.

Remove the cakes from oven; let cool in cans on a wire rack. When cool, remove from the cans.

Makes 2 quick breads

Whole Wheat Chocolate Banana Bread

I have always thought banana bread was better with some whole wheat flour in it to add texture, and now I think it is even tastier with chocolate. I added grated chocolate to my best banana bread and it turned out to be supermoist, with subtle chocolate flavor flecks through and through. It is good and good for you.

Softened butter for greasing the pan
¼ cup plus 1 tablespoon all-purpose flour
¼ cup whole wheat flour
½ teaspoon baking powder
¼ teaspoon baking soda
⅛ teaspoon salt
1½ ounces bittersweet chocolate, grated
½ cup mashed ripe banana, about ½ large banana
¼ cup plus 2 tablespoons firmly packed light brown sugar
2 tablespoons vegetable oil
1½ tablespoons well-beaten egg
¾ teaspoon pure vanilla extract
¼ cup chopped pecans or walnuts, optional

Position a rack in the center of the oven and preheat the oven to 350°F. Lightly butter a petite loaf pan (2-cup capacity, about 5 × 3 inches). Set the pan aside.

Place the flours, baking powder, baking soda, and salt in a medium bowl; whisk to blend the dry ingredients. Sprinkle the grated chocolate on the flour mixture, and toss with a fork until well combined. Make a well in the center of the mixture.

Place the banana, brown sugar, oil, egg, and vanilla in a small bowl; stir to blend well. Add to the flour mixture and stir just until blended. Stir in the walnuts, if using.

Pour the batter into the prepared loaf pan. Bake until a toothpick inserted in the center comes out clean, 30 to 32 minutes.

Remove the pan from the oven and let it cool on a wire rack for 10 minutes. Then remove the bread from the pan and let it cool, upright, on the rack. Serve warm or at room temperature. (The loaf may be wrapped in aluminum foil, placed in a plastic freezer bag, and frozen up to 1 month.)

Makes 1 loaf, 4 or 5 slices

Chocolate Orange Flan

I like flan custard to show a clean, glassy cut when a bite is spooned out of it, proving that it is lighter in texture from using milk instead of cream. This one does that from the chocolate milk. The custard tastes sweet enough from the milk and the liqueur or juice concentrate, without added sugar; there is enough caramelized sugar in the light syrup that cradles the custard.

This recipe makes a little extra caramelized sugar; some goes into the flan dishes and the rest is spread out and hardened into brittle, which you can break up and sprinkle on top for garnish.

⅔ cup sugar
¾ cup chocolate milk
2 teaspoons Cointreau or frozen orange juice concentrate
1 ounce bittersweet chocolate, finely chopped
¼ ounce unsweetened chocolate, finely chopped
1 large egg
1 large egg yolk
1 teaspoon pure vanilla extract

Position a rack in the center of the oven and preheat the oven to 325°F. Place two 1-cup soufflé dishes or ramekins in an 8- or 9-inch square baking pan for easier handling. Set the pan aside.

Place the sugar and ½ cup water in a small, heavy saucepan; bring to a boil over medium-high heat, stirring constantly until the sugar dissolves. Then boil, without stirring, until the color turns golden amber, 12 to 13 minutes.

Carefully spoon 2 tablespoons of the caramel into each soufflé dish. Pour the remaining caramel onto a silicone baking pan liner or a sheet of lightly buttered aluminum foil. Let it stand at room temperature until the sheet of caramel hardens, about 20 minutes.

Place the chocolate milk, liqueur or orange juice concentrate, and both chocolates in the saucepan; bring it to a simmer, stirring until the chocolate melts and the mixture is smooth.

Place the egg, egg yolk, and vanilla in a bowl; whisk until the mixture is blended. While you are continuing to whisk, gradually pour in the hot milk mixture and blend in well. Pour the custard into the caramel-coated soufflé dishes. Pour enough hot water into the baking pan to come halfway up the sides of the dishes. Cover the entire baking pan tightly with aluminum foil.

Bake until the flans are just set, 35 to 40 minutes. Carefully remove the soufflé dishes from the hot water in the baking pan, lifting them carefully with a flat, slotted, metal spatula. Refrigerate them, uncovered, until cooled. Then cover them and refrigerate until cold, about 6 hours or overnight.

To serve, run a small sharp knife around the inside of the soufflé dishes to loosen the flans. Cover a soufflé dish with a dessert plate, and quickly invert the flan onto the plate. Pour and scrape the caramel mixture remaining in the soufflé dish over the flan. Unmold the remaining flan as before. Break up the cooled caramel and garnish the flans with the caramel shards.

Makes 2 flans

HOLIDAY DECADENCE
More Goodies You Cannot Live Without

❧

*D*uring the years after I flew the family coop, there were times I could not get to my parents' house for the big dinner. So I would practice roasting turkey, making dressing, and baking pies or cakes myself. I sometimes had eight people at my table that, like me, deemed it impractical to make the trip home; but more often there were just two or three of us. I was always faced with the challenge of creating a large, multi-course holiday dinner . . . in small batches.

When I got married, before my husband and I had our children, that need to reduce family size portions of everything came up again. We might have been able to join a large gathering of family, but we did not necessarily want to . . . we were nesting, after all.

But, not once during the years when it was just the two of us for mealtime, did I consider leaving out the chocolate pumpkin pie or Santa-shaped chocolate sugar cookies. I am a hopeless chocoholic and holiday romantic to boot. The jubilation of the season simply took over, and I baked regardless of how many people were consuming my goodies.

Now, however, I know how to bake in small batches, so I can make holiday goodies often, and in appropriate quantities. There can be a new, different batch of cookies each day during a holiday break. And I can make three different miniature pies and tarts if I choose to, knowing that I do not have to contend with massive quantities of leftovers. Baking in small batches is quite freeing, actually. You can have your cake, pie, cookies, or breads and eat them all, too—no guilt attached!

Chocolate Orange Truffle Tarts

These shiny glazed tarts are a beautiful Christmas or New Year's Eve dessert. They are intensely flavored, and just a little Cointreau adds silky orange elegance to the smooth truffle filling. Candied orange slices are a beautiful decoration.

2 partially baked Rich Sweet Pastry shells (page 122), baked in 4½ × ¾-inch tart pans with removable bottoms, still in the pans

For the filling
¼ cup heavy (whipping) cream
1 tablespoon Cointreau
Pinch of salt
2 ounces bittersweet chocolate, chopped
1½ tablespoons beaten egg yolk (about 1½ yolks)

For the glaze
1½ tablespoons heavy (whipping) cream
½ teaspoon light corn syrup
¾ ounce bittersweet chocolate, chopped
2 teaspoons warm water
Candied Oranges (recipe follows)

Position a rack in the center of the oven and preheat the oven to 350°F. Place the tart pans on a baking sheet for easier handling and set it aside.

Prepare the filling: Bring the cream, liqueur, and salt to a simmer in a small saucepan. Place the chocolate in a bowl; pour the hot cream mixture over the chocolate in the bowl. Let it stand 1 minute, then stir until smooth. Place the beaten egg yolk in a small bowl; whisk some of the hot mixture into the egg yolk, then whisk the egg yolk mixture into the remaining hot mixture. Pour into the pastry shells. Bake until the filling in each tart is set about an inch from the edge but still jiggly in the center, about 20 minutes; the centers will continue to set as the tart cools. Transfer the tarts to a wire rack and let them cool completely, about 1 hour.

Prepare the glaze: Place the cream and corn syrup in a small, microwave-safe bowl; microwave on high power until very hot, about 20 seconds. Add the chocolate; let it stand 1 minute, swirling the cream to submerge the chocolate. Stir until smooth; stir in the warm water.

Pour the glaze over the tarts, swirling them to allow the glaze to flow and coat the tops evenly. Refrigerate the tarts until ready to serve, at least 1 hour.

Remove the tarts from the pans; cut the Candied Oranges into quarters and arrange over the tarts to garnish.

Makes 2 tarts

Candied Oranges
1 cup water
1 cup sugar
1 small, thin-skinned orange, very thinly sliced and seeded

Bring the water and sugar to a boil in a large, heavy skillet, stirring until the sugar dissolves. Add the orange slices in a single layer to the skillet using tongs. Reduce the heat to medium-low and simmer 30 to 40 minutes, or until the white pith of orange becomes translucent, turning slices occasionally. Remove from heat; allow the orange slices to cool in the syrup, turning occasionally.

Bittersweet Truffle Tarts with Salted Pistachio Brittle

For the December 1999 issue of *Bon Appétit* magazine, I wrote a dessert feature story that included spectacular desserts that you would want to serve for the last course of the millennium. I developed a chocolate tart much like this one and a vanilla pear cheesecake with similar pistachio shards standing up in it that reflected light like pieces of amber glass. Arrange the shards in an irregular pattern on their edges—just deep enough through the tops of the silky chocolate to make them stand up. It forms a beautiful presentation, and the pistachios in their very thin, clear golden casing make a sophisticated candy brittle.

Prepare Chocolate Orange Truffle Tarts (page 281) omitting Cointreau in the filling and adding 1 tablespoon heavy cream instead. Omit the candied oranges. Stand shards of Pistachio Brittle up in tarts, or chop and sprinkle in tarts.

Salted Pistachio Brittle

Thin sheets of crispy caramel candy studded with salted roasted pistachios add a splash of design when you stand them up in a dessert. You can also crush the homemade brittle and sprinkle it on desserts.

Nonstick cooking spray
¼ cup sugar
1 tablespoon water
Pinch of sea salt
2 tablespoons salted roasted shelled pistachios

Lightly coat a baking sheet with cooking spray and set it aside.

Place the sugar, water, and sea salt in a small, heavy saucepan over medium-high heat; bring to a boil, stirring with a fork until the sugar dissolves. Boil the sugar syrup until it is golden amber in color, swirling the saucepan occasionally. Remove from the heat.

Working quickly, stir the pistachios into the caramel and immediately pour the mixture onto the prepared baking sheet. Press the tip of a table knife into the edges of the caramel, nudging and stretching it gently in all directions to form a very thin sheet. Let the brittle cool completely.

Break the brittle into irregular shards.

Makes about ½ cup pieces

Chocolate Cranberry Truffle Tarts

These tarts are a festive combination of flavors; the cranberry liqueur adds a sweet-tart flavor. Alternately, you can use reduced cranberry juice: boil ⅔ cup cranberry juice and 1 tablespoon sugar in a small saucepan down to 3 tablespoons. The concentrated juice will give you powerful cranberry flavor, too. Use 1 tablespoon of the reduced juice in the glaze in place of the liqueur.

Cranberry Crystals make a gorgeous garnish. Each berry or cluster of berries is encased in a crystallized sugar shell, with swirling strands of ruby-colored spun sugar attached. Make the garnish no more than 1 hour before serving.

2 partially baked Rich Sweet Pastry shells (page 122), baked in 4½ × ¾-inch
tart pans with removable bottoms, still in the pans

For the filling
3 tablespoons heavy (whipping) cream
2 tablespoons cranberry liqueur or reduced cranberry syrup
Pinch of salt
2 ounces bittersweet chocolate, chopped
1½ tablespoons beaten egg yolk (about 1½ yolks)

For the glaze
4 teaspoons heavy (whipping) cream
½ teaspoon light corn syrup
¾ ounce bittersweet chocolate, chopped

1 tablespoon cranberry liqueur, reduced cranberry syrup, or water
Cranberry Crystals (recipe follows)

Position a rack in the center of the oven and preheat the oven to 350°F. Place tart pans on a baking sheet for easier handling and set it aside.

Prepare the filling: Bring the cream, liqueur, and salt to a simmer in a small saucepan. Place the chopped chocolate in a bowl; pour the hot cream mixture over the chocolate. Let it stand 1 minute, then stir until smooth.

Place the beaten egg yolk in a small bowl; whisk some of the hot mixture into the egg yolk, then whisk the egg yolk mixture into the remaining hot mixture. Pour the filling into the pastry shells. Bake until the filling in each tart is set about an inch from the edge but still jiggly in the center, 10 to 12 minutes; the centers will continue to set as the tarts cool. Transfer the tarts to a wire rack and let them cool completely, about 1 hour.

Prepare the glaze: Place the cream and corn syrup in a small, microwave-safe bowl; microwave on high power until very hot, about 20 seconds. Add the chopped chocolate; let it stand 1 minute, swirling the cream to submerge the chocolate. Stir until smooth; stir in the 1 tablespoon liqueur.

Pour the glaze over the tarts, swirling them to allow the glaze to flow and coat the tops evenly. Refrigerate until ready to serve, at least 1 hour.

Remove the tarts from pans; garnish with the Cranberry Crystals.

Makes 2 tarts

Cranberry Crystals
⅓ cup fresh or thawed frozen cranberries
¼ cup sugar

Line a cooling rack with paper towels. Separate the cranberries on the paper towels and let them air-dry thoroughly, turning them occasionally, about 1 to 2 hours for thawed frozen cranberries.

Line a baking sheet with nonstick aluminum foil. Place the dried berries close together on the foil and set aside.

Place the sugar and 2 teaspoons of water in a small saucepan and bring to a boil over medium heat, stirring constantly until the sugar melts, 3 to 4 minutes. Boil for 2 minutes, without stirring, then pour the melted sugar evenly over the cranberries. Do not toss the berries. Working quickly and using two forks, separate the berries into single berries and clusters of three, pulling the sugar between them into strands as you go. Let the crystal berries cool completely before using them.

Makes about ½ cup, for two desserts

∾

Southern Pecan and Chocolate Chip Pies

Southern Comfort is a New Orleans tradition, and is so good in these pecan pies. You can do without it, or substitute Irish whiskey, but the combination of fruit, spices, and whiskey is the *lagniappe*—and adds a Cajun lilt. Any way you make it, with or without, they are delicious.

> 2 partially baked Basic Pastry shells (page 118), baked in 4 × 1⅜-inch tart
>   pans with removable bottoms, still in the pans
> ½ cup plus 1 tablespoon sugar
> 1 large egg
> ¼ cup dark or light corn syrup
> 1 tablespoon Southern Comfort, optional
> 2 teaspoons unsalted butter, melted
> ½ teaspoon pure vanilla extract
> Pinch of salt
> 3 tablespoons semisweet chocolate chips
> ⅓ cup pecan halves

Position a rack in the center of the oven and preheat the oven to 350°F. Put the pastry shells in the tart pans on a baking sheet for easier handling and set it aside.

Place the sugar, egg, corn syrup, liquor (if using), melted butter, vanilla, and salt in a medium bowl and whisk until the mixture is smooth and blended.

Sprinkle the chocolate chips over the bottoms of the pastry shells, dividing them evenly. Pour the filling evenly over the chocolate chips. Arrange the pecan halves on top of the filling, dividing them evenly.

Bake the pies until the filling is just set in the center. Let them cool until lukewarm on a wire rack. Then carefully remove the tarts from the pans and place them on serving plates. Serve warm with ice cream or whipped cream.

Makes 2 tarts

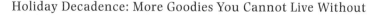

Chocolate Derby Pecan Tarts

When I performed Southern Living Cooking Schools, we demonstrated a particularly good Kentucky Derby Pie. Derby pies are pecan pies with bourbon in them, and legend has it that some gentleman spilled his bourbon in the pecan pie. This small-batch version is just like it, only better with chocolate melted all the way through.

2 partially baked Basic Pastry shells (page 118), baked in 4½ × 1-inch tart
    pans with removable bottoms, still in the pans
1 ounce unsweetened chocolate, chopped
1 teaspoon unsalted butter
⅓ cup sugar
3 tablespoons light corn syrup
1 tablespoon bourbon
1 teaspoon pure vanilla extract
Pinch of salt
1 large egg
⅓ cup chopped pecans, toasted
Bourbon Whipped Cream (recipe follows)

Position a rack in the center of the oven and preheat the oven to 350°F. Put the pastry shells in the tart pans on a baking sheet for easier handling and set it aside.

Place the chocolate and butter in a small glass bowl; microwave at medium power until the chocolate is soft and the butter is just melted, about 1 to 1¼ minutes. Stir the chocolate mixture until it is smooth. Let it cool.

Whisk together the sugar, corn syrup, bourbon, vanilla, salt, and egg in a medium bowl. Pour the filling into the prepared pastry shells and sprinkle with the pecans. Bake until the edges of the pies are slightly puffed and the centers are soft but set, 25 to 30 minutes. Remove the baking sheet from the oven and transfer the pies to a wire rack. Let them stand until they are cool enough to handle, then remove the pies from the tart pans. Serve them warm or at room temperature with Bourbon Whipped Cream.

Makes 2 tarts

Bourbon Whipped Cream
⅓ cup cold heavy (whipping) cream
2 tablespoons confectioners' sugar
1 tablespoon bourbon

Place the ingredients in a small, deep mixing bowl. Beat with a handheld electric mixer on high speed until firm peaks form, about 1 minute.

Makes about ⅔ cup

ᳰ

Chocolate Pumpkin Pies

The bittersweet chocolate here forms a shell around the silky traditional pumpkin pie filling, so it does not interfere with the pumpkin taste but rather accents it. The pair makes a beautiful harvest table pie.

> 2 partially baked Basic Pastry shells (page 118), baked in 4 × 1⅜-inch
>   tart pans with removable bottoms, still in the pans
> 1 ounce fine-quality bittersweet chocolate, finely chopped
>
> **For the filling**
> ¼ cup cold heavy (whipping) cream
> 1½ ounces fine-quality bittersweet chocolate, chopped
> ¼ cup canned pure pumpkin puree (not pumpkin pie filling)
> 2 tablespoons firmly packed dark brown sugar
> 1 teaspoon all-purpose flour
> ¼ teaspoon pumpkin pie spice
> Pinch of salt
> 1½ tablespoons well-beaten egg
> 1 ounce milk chocolate, melted

Position a rack in the center of the oven and preheat the oven to 400°F. Put the pastry shells in the tart pans on a baking sheet for easier handling. Sprinkle the chopped chocolate in the bottoms of the pastry shells, and place in the oven to melt the chocolate, about 2 minutes. Spread the melted chocolate on bottoms and up the sides of the pastry shells with the back of a spoon. Let the chocolate coating cool completely. Reduce the oven temperature to 325°F.

Make the filling: Place the cream in a microwave-safe bowl; microwave on high power until simmering, about 20 seconds. Add the chocolate; let stand 1 minute to soften, then stir the mixture until it is smooth. Whisk in the pumpkin puree, brown sugar, flour, pumpkin pie spice, and salt; whisk in the egg. Pour the filling into the prepared pastry shells, dividing it evenly. Bake the pies until the filling is just set in the center, about 25 minutes.

Remove the baking sheet from the oven and transfer the pies to a wire rack. Let the pies cool completely; serve at room temperature or cover and refrigerate until well chilled, at least 4 hours. Before serving, dip the tines of a fork in the melted milk chocolate and drizzle over the pies.

Makes 2 pies

❧

Chocolate Pumpkin Ginger Cheesecakes

I splurge on champagne to serve with these beauties. The subtly spiced cheesecakes sparkle with shards of Candied Ginger Brittle as decorations to catch the light.

For the crust

Unsalted butter for greasing the cans

¼ cup chopped pecans, ground

¼ cup shortbread cookie crumbs

1 tablespoon firmly packed light brown sugar

1 tablespoon plus 2 teaspoons unsalted butter,
   melted

For the filling

2½ ounces fine-quality milk chocolate

5 ounces cream cheese, at room temperature

¼ cup firmly packed light brown sugar

1 large egg, lightly beaten

2 large egg yolks

¼ cup plus 1 tablespoon canned pure pumpkin puree
   (not pumpkin pie filling)

1 teaspoon all-purpose flour

¼ teaspoon ground ginger

⅛ teaspoon ground cardamom

Pinch of salt

For the topping

2 ounces milk chocolate, chopped

3 tablespoons heavy (whipping) cream

Candied Ginger Brittle (recipe follows)

Preheat the oven to 325°F. Lightly butter the insides of two 8-ounce cans. Place the cans on a piece of parchment paper and trace around the circumference. Cut out two parchment rounds and line bottoms of the cans with them. Cut out two 11 × 2-inch strips of parchment paper, and use them to line the inside of each can; the parchment paper should reach the top of the cans. Place the cans in an 8- to 9-inch square baking pan and set the pan aside.

Make the crust: Place the pecans, cookie crumbs, and brown sugar in a small bowl. Stir in the melted butter until the crumbs are evenly moistened. Spoon the crumb mixture into the prepared cans, dividing it evenly. Gently press the crumb mixture down with your fingertips. Bake until the color of the crust begins to darken, 8 to 10 minutes.

Remove the baking pan from the oven and transfer it with the cans onto a wire rack to cool. Keep the oven on.

Make the filling: Place the chopped milk chocolate in a microwave-safe bowl; microwave on medium power until soft, about 1½ minutes. Stir until the chocolate is smooth. Let it cool.

Place the cream cheese and brown sugar in a medium mixing bowl and beat with a handheld electric mixer on medium speed just until the mixture is smooth and creamy. Add the egg and the egg yolks; reduce the mixer speed to low, and beat just until it is blended into the cream cheese mixture, about 10 seconds. Beat in the pumpkin puree, flour, spices, and salt on low speed just until the mixture is smooth. Beat in the melted, cooled chocolate on low speed just until blended.

Pour the batter into the prepared cans, dividing it evenly. Pour boiling water into the baking pan to come halfway up the sides of the cans. Bake until the cheesecakes are just set, 30 to 33 minutes. Remove the baking pan from the oven; transfer the cans to a wire rack, and let them cool completely. Cover and refrigerate the cheesecakes for 6 hours or overnight.

Prepare the topping: Place the chopped chocolate in a small bowl. Bring 3 tablespoons cream to a boil in a small saucepan. Pour the hot cream over the chocolate and let stand 1 minute, then stir until it is smooth. Pour the chocolate over the cheesecakes; refrigerate the cheesecakes until the chocolate sets, about 30 minutes.

To serve, run a sharp knife around the sides of the cans to loosen the cheesecakes. Turn the cakes out, remove the parchment paper, and place them, upright, on serving plates. Garnish with Candied Ginger Brittle. The cheesecakes will keep, covered, in the refrigerator for 1 week.

Makes 2 cheesecakes

Candied Ginger Brittle
Nonstick cooking spray
¼ cup sugar
2 tablespoons minced candied (crystallized)
    ginger

Butter a tablespoon. Set it aside.

Lightly coat a baking sheet with cooking spray. Place the sugar and 1 tablespoon of water in a small, heavy saucepan. Bring to a boil over medium-high heat, stirring with a fork until the sugar dissolves. Then boil, swirling the saucepan occasionally, until the syrup is a golden amber color, 3 to 4 minutes. Immediately remove the pan from the heat.

Working quickly, stir the candied ginger into the caramel with the buttered spoon and then immediately pour the mixture onto the prepared baking sheet. Press the tip of the spoon into the edges of the caramel, nudging and stretching it gently in all directions to form a very thin sheet and to separate the ginger pieces. Let the brittle cool completely, about 15 minutes.

Break the brittle into irregular shards. (Store in an airtight container at room temperature for up to 2 days.)

Makes about ¼ cup, or enough to garnish two cheesecakes

Cranberry Chocolate Roulade

I once pitched a cranberries and chocolate story to a major food magazine, and ended up writing a story about holiday chocolate dessert flavor pairings, namely that one, as well as pear and pistachio, hazelnuts and dried cherries, and others. For me, chocolate and cranberries were the bomb. In this recipe, the cranberries are essentially dried in the oven with sugar, so they are concentrated in flavor and sweetened. They end up looking like plump raisins, and they are rolled up in the chocolate cake with the filling. The thick, sweet-tart juices that collect as the cranberries bake go into the chocolate cream filling and frosting, and the flavor is intense and fruity.

For the candied cranberries
¾ cup fresh or frozen whole cranberries
⅔ cup plus 1 teaspoon sugar, divided

For the cake
Unsalted butter for greasing the pan
1 large egg yolk
4 tablespoons confectioners' sugar, divided
1 teaspoon very hot water
½ teaspoon pure vanilla extract
1 tablespoon cake flour
2 teaspoons unsweetened cocoa powder
Pinch of salt
2 large eggs whites, at room temperature
⅛ teaspoon cream of tartar
Additional confectioners' sugar

For the filling and frosting
1 ounce bittersweet chocolate, finely chopped
¼ cup cold heavy (whipping) cream
1 tablespoon reserved cranberry liquid
Rich Chocolate Cranberry Frosting (recipe follows)

Make the candied cranberries: Preheat the oven to 350°F. Butter a 9 × 5-inch loaf pan and add the cranberries to the pan. Sprinkle ⅔ cup of the sugar over the cranberries; cover the loaf pan tightly with aluminum foil. Bake until the cranberries are shriveled like plump raisins and the juices are syrupy, about 1 hour, stirring once after 30 minutes. Protecting your hands with oven mitts, carefully pour off the mixture through a fine-mesh sieve, reserving the juices in a glass bowl; you should have about 1½ tablespoons syrup. Set it aside for the Rich Chocolate Cranberry Frosting. Spoon the cranberries on a piece of wax paper and let cool completely. Sprinkle with the remaining 1 teaspoon sugar. Clean the loaf pan.

Make the cake: Position a rack in the center of the oven and preheat the oven to 350°F. Butter and flour the loaf pan and line the bottom lengthwise and up the short ends with a piece of parchment paper. Set the pan aside.

Place the egg yolk, 3 tablespoons of the confectioners' sugar, and the hot water in a small, deep mixing bowl. Beat with a handheld electric mixer on high speed until the mixture is pale and has thickened, 1½ to 2 minutes; when you turn off the mixer and lift a beater, a ribbon of egg mixture should drizzle back onto the remainder in the bowl and leave a "track" that sits on the top before it sinks in. Beat in the vanilla. Sift the flour, cocoa powder, and salt over the batter. Fold it in gently with a rubber spatula.

Wash the mixer beaters and dry them thoroughly. Place the egg whites and cream of tartar in a medium mixing bowl and beat with a handheld mixer on medium speed until foamy, about 15 seconds. Sprinkle the remaining

1 tablespoon of confectioners' sugar over the egg whites and beat until firm peaks form. Fold the beaten egg whites into the yolk mixture, making sure no streaks of white remain.

Spoon the batter into the prepared pan, and smooth the top with a rubber spatula. Bake until a toothpick inserted in the center comes out clean, 12 to 13 minutes.

While the cake is baking, lay a 13-inch-long sheet of parchment paper on the counter and sift the confectioners' sugar into an area the size of the baking pan. As soon as the cake has finished baking, invert the pan over the sugared area and lift off the pan; peel off the parchment paper that lines the cake layer.

Fold one end of the long sheet of parchment paper over a short end of the cake, and roll up the cake in the parchment paper. Place the roll, seam side down, on a wire rack to cool.

Make the filling: Put the chocolate in a microwave-safe bowl; microwave on medium power until soft, 1 to 1½ minutes. Stir until smooth, and then let the chocolate cool to room temperature. The chocolate should be cooled but still soft.

Place the cream in a small, deep mixing bowl and beat with a handheld electric mixer on high speed until firm peaks form. Beat in the melted, cooled chocolate just until blended.

When the cake has cooled, unroll it. Spread the filling on the cake to within 1 inch of the edges. Arrange the candied cranberries over the filling. Roll up the cake, beginning with a short end and using the parchment paper to help; do not roll the parchment paper into the cake. Place the cake roll, seam side down, on a serving platter and frost it with the Rich Chocolate Cranberry Frosting. Let the cake stand for 1 hour before serving.

Makes 1 cake roll, 3 to 4 slices

Rich Chocolate Cranberry Frosting
¼ cup heavy (whipping) cream
Reserved cranberry liquid
Pinch of salt
1½ ounces fine-quality bittersweet or semisweet chocolate, finely chopped
1½ ounces fine-quality milk chocolate, finely chopped

Place the cream, reserved cranberry liquid, and salt in a microwave-safe bowl; microwave on high power until the cream simmers, about 40 seconds. Add both chocolates and swirl to immerse the chocolate in the hot cream. Let the mixture stand until the chocolate is softened, 1 minute; then stir until smooth. Refrigerate the frosting to allow it to harden until it is firm enough to spread, stirring it every 5 minutes, about 20 minutes.

Makes ½ cup

❧

Chocolate Sugar Cookies

This is the nicest cookie dough; it is soft and easy to roll, and holds its shape well no matter what type of cutters you use. So the cookies bake up well for every holiday season. They are lovely glazed with tinted royal icing. And the cookies are festive when you sprinkle the icing, while it is wet, with minced candied ginger, finely chopped nuts, and decorative candies.

You can sandwich two together with Ganache Cookie Filling (recipe follows), or decorate the tops of the cookies with it. To make pistachio trees, cut out the cookies with tree-shaped cutters, spread Ganache Cookie Filling over the cookies, and sprinkle them with finely chopped pistachios.

> 1 ounce semisweet chocolate, chopped
> ½ cup plus 1 tablespoon all-purpose flour
> ¼ teaspoon baking powder
> ⅛ teaspoon salt
> 3 tablespoons unsalted butter, softened
> ¼ cup confectioners' sugar
> 1 tablespoon well-beaten egg
> ½ teaspoon pure vanilla extract
> Royal Icing (recipe follows)
> Ganache Cookie Filling (recipe follows)

Place the chocolate in a small, microwave-safe bowl; microwave on medium power until soft, about 1 minute. Stir until smooth. Let cool.

Place the flour, baking powder, and salt in a fine-mesh sieve, sift into a bowl or onto a piece of waxed paper.

Place the butter and confectioners' sugar in a medium mixing bowl and beat with a handheld electric mixer on medium speed until well blended, about 20 seconds. Beat in the cooled chocolate until blended, about 15 seconds. Beat in the egg and vanilla just until blended. Add the flour mixture and beat until the dough is well combined, about 20 seconds, scraping the bowl as necessary.

Shape the dough into a disk and roll it out between two sheets of wax paper to ¼-inch thickness. Place the wax paper, with the dough, on a baking sheet and place in the refrigerator until chilled, at least 30 minutes.

Place a rack in the center of the oven and preheat the oven to 350°F. Line a baking sheet with parchment paper and set it aside.

Cut out the cookies using 2- or 3-inch cutters, and transfer them to the prepared baking sheet. Reroll and cut out the dough scraps. Bake the cookies until firm and beginning to darken at the edges, 10 to 11 minutes. Slide the parchment paper, with the cookies, onto a wire rack and let them cool completely. Use a metal spatula to lift the cookies from the parchment paper.

Either leave the Royal Icing white or divide it among as many bowls as you have food colors, and tint the icing as desired, using separate toothpicks to dip into each jar of food color and then into the bowls of icing. Stir the tinted icings well. If necessary, thin the icing with water, ¼ teaspoon at a time, until it is thin enough to brush over the cookies in a thin layer. Use a pastry brush to spread the icing over the cookies. If you like, decorate the tops with colored candy decorations while the icing is still wet. Or pipe contrasting colors of icing on the glazed cookies. Let the cookies dry on a wire rack until they are firm, at least 4 hours.

Makes 10 cookies

Royal Icing

2½ cups confectioners' sugar

1 tablespoon plus 1 teaspoon pasteurized powdered egg whites,
  such as Just Whites

Place the confectioners' sugar and powdered egg whites in a large bowl and whisk to blend them well. Whisk in 3 tablespoons of water, stirring until the icing is very smooth. If necessary, adjust the thickness by whisking in additional water by teaspoonfuls, or additional confectioners' sugar by tablespoonfuls, until the icing is medium thick. Use the icing before it hardens, usually 15 to 30 minutes after it is made.

Makes enough icing for 8 to 10 cookies

Ganache Cookie Filling

1 ounce bittersweet or semisweet chocolate, chopped

1 tablespoon plus 1 teaspoon heavy (whipping) cream

½ tablespoon light corn syrup

1 tablespoon crème fraîche or sour cream

Place the chocolate in a small bowl. Place the cream and corn syrup in a microwave-safe bowl; microwave on high power until simmering, about 30 seconds. Pour over the chocolate and let stand 1 minute. Stir until smooth. Stir in the crème fraîche. Refrigerate until thick and spreadable, 20 to 30 minutes.

Makes about ¼ cup

Peppermint White Chocolate Shortbread Cookies

If you only make one Christmas cookie recipe, let this be it. The dough is really easy to work with and the cookies hold their shapes well while they bake. They are tender but sturdy, and they make gorgeous candy cane shapes.

2 ounces fine-quality white chocolate, divided, chopped

½ cup all-purpose flour

1 tablespoon plus 1 teaspoon cornstarch

Pinch of salt

⅛ teaspoon freshly grated nutmeg

3½ tablespoons unsalted butter, softened

3 tablespoons confectioners' sugar

1 teaspoon pure vanilla extract

¼ teaspoon solid vegetable shortening

¼ cup crushed hard peppermint candy

Position a rack in the center of the oven and preheat the oven to 350°F. Line a baking sheet with parchment paper and set it aside.

Place 1 ounce of the white chocolate in a small, microwave-safe bowl; microwave on medium power until it is soft, about 1 minute. Stir until smooth. Let cool to room temperature.

Place the flour, cornstarch, salt, and nutmeg in a bowl, and whisk to blend.

Place the butter, confectioners' sugar, and vanilla in a small, deep mixing bowl and beat with a handheld electric mixer on medium speed until well blended, about 20 seconds. Beat in the melted white chocolate. Add the flour mixture and beat at low speed until dough is blended.

Turn the dough out onto a piece of wax paper. Flatten it into a disk and refrigerate the dough 1 hour.

Roll the dough out to a ½-inch thickness on a floured board. Cut out the cookies, using 2- to 3-inch cutters. Transfer the cookies to the prepared baking sheet, spacing them ½ inch apart. Gather and reroll the scraps; cut out additional cookies and transfer to baking sheet. Bake the cookies until firm to touch and just beginning to color, 10 to 12 minutes.

Remove the baking sheet from the oven, and slide the parchment paper, with the cookies, onto a wire rack and let them cool completely. Use a metal spatula to lift the cookies off the parchment paper.

When the cookies are cool, chop the remaining 1 ounce white chocolate and place it in a small, microwave-safe bowl; microwave on medium power until soft, about 1 minute. Stir until smooth. Stir in the shortening.

Brush the white chocolate mixture over half of each cookie, and let stand until cool but not set, about 10 minutes. While the white chocolate is still soft, sprinkle the crushed candy over the white chocolate. Let the cookies stand until coating is hard.

Makes 6 to 8 cookies

၄၅

Hazelnut Sachertorte Bars

A true sachertorte is made of dense chocolate cake layers, apricot preserves, and chocolate ganache. These bars are a take-off of the Viennese dessert; I have topped a buttery hazelnut cookie layer with apricot preserves and a lightly sweet brownie layer, then drizzled laces of melted semisweet and white chocolates over the cooled bars. They are absolute decadence, and they make a lovely dessert with a steaming cup of dark roast coffee.

For the cookie layer

¼ cup hazelnuts, toasted, skins removed

3 tablespoons all-purpose flour

3 tablespoons confectioners' sugar

1½ tablespoons unsalted butter, softened

1 teaspoon well-beaten egg

For the chocolate layer

2 tablespoons sieved apricot preserves

2 tablespoons unsalted butter

1 ounce bittersweet chocolate, chopped

2 tablespoons granulated sugar

1 tablespoon well-beaten egg

2½ tablespoons all-purpose flour

Pinch of salt

½ teaspoon pure vanilla extract

1 ounce semisweet chocolate, melted

½ ounce white chocolate, melted

Position the rack in the center of the oven and preheat the oven to 350°F. Line a 5 × 3-inch loaf pan (2-cup capacity) with aluminum foil, pressing the foil into the corners and up the sides of the loaf pan and extending the foil 1½ inches over the edges of the pan. Lightly butter the foil. Set the pan aside.

Make the cookie layer: Place the hazelnuts, 3 tablespoons of the all-purpose flour, and confectioners' sugar in a food processor fitted with the knife blade; process until the nuts are ground. Add the softened butter and 1 teaspoon beaten egg and pulse until mixture starts to clump together, 11 or 12 pulses. Press the mixture into the loaf pan. Bake until beginning to brown, about 15 minutes. Let cool on a wire rack. Turn the oven off.

When the crust has cooled, spread the preserves over the crust. Preheat the oven again to 350°F.

Make the chocolate layer: Place the 2 tablespoons butter and chopped chocolate in a small, microwave-safe bowl; microwave until soft, about 1½ minutes. Stir until smooth. Let cool 10 minutes. Whisk in the sugar, then 1 tablespoon beaten egg. Stir in the flour and salt. Stir in vanilla. Pour the mixture over the apricot preserves layer.

Bake until the chocolate layer is just set and a toothpick inserted into the center of the chocolate layer comes out clean, about 20 minutes. Let cool completely in the pan on a wire rack. When completely cool, drizzle with the melted semisweet chocolate. Refrigerate 10 minutes to harden. Drizzle the melted white chocolate over the semisweet chocolate layer. Refrigerate 10 minutes to harden. Lift the brownie layer from the pan and peel the foil from the sides. Cut into bars.

Makes 3 to 4 bars

❧

LIQUID PLEASURES
Sumptuous Drinks for Fun and Frolic

෬

I believe a book about chocolate should include the best hot chocolate ever, and this chapter has it (The Just Plain Fabulous Hot Chocolate)! There are also other flavor variations to suit your moods . . . Accompanying the classic hot chocolate, there is a coconut creamy dark chocolate version and a vanilla-scented one made with Chai and white chocolate. All three will make you sigh with pleasure.

If it's something cool and refreshing you're in the mood for, you do not have to be a child to enjoy these home-style milk shakes and the frozen yogurt smoothie. All are ice cream parlor delights—Chocolate and Peanut Butter, Chocolate Malt, and Raspberry and Chocolate. The raspberry variation has a dash of Chambord to intensify the flavor and enjoyment; the peanut butter flavor is just downright liquid candy. And the retro, thick chocolate malted shake will send you back through a time warp—right to a booth at the malt shop.

And, ah, the Chocolate Martini. . . . Purely an adult extravagance, it is shaken and poured into glasses rimmed creatively with cocoa powder, nuts, or chocolate syrup. The cocktails are garnished with chocolate truffles or fruit that matches the liqueur you choose to add to the chocolate liqueur and vodka. I have a collection of fun artisan martini glasses that I use to serve this extraordinary cocktail for two.

Just Plain Fabulous Hot Chocolate

When I tested this on my daughter and two of her eight-year-old peers, they all said that it needed to taste richer and thicker, even as they drank it down saying, "Oh, this is so good," every time their lips touched their cups.

So I made some adjustments, and when they said it was right, I let a few adults have a go at it. I served brandy and assorted liqueurs with theirs and let them add according to taste. We all agreed that the plain hot chocolate was so rich in flavor from the marshmallow creme and good quality chocolate that it needed hardly any sugar. And a little alcohol didn't hurt, either.

1 cup whole milk
1¼ ounces bittersweet chocolate, chopped
¼ ounce unsweetened chocolate, chopped
1 tablespoon sugar, or to taste
2 tablespoons Marshmallow Creme, such as Kraft Jet-Puffed
Pinch of kosher salt
½ teaspoon pure vanilla extract
Brandy or assorted liqueurs, optional
Cinnamon sticks, optional
Marshmallows, optional

Heat 2 mugs by filling them with very hot tap water; let the mugs stand until they feel warm to the touch, 1 to 2 minutes. Pour out the water.

HOMEMADE CHOCOLATE SYRUP

this syrup is much better than anything you can buy, and it is so easy. I keep a jar in the fridge at all times, ready to go on ice cream, dip cookies into, and stir into recipes.

½ cup half-and-half
½ cup (3 ounces) semisweet or bittersweet chocolate chips
2 tablespoons sugar
1 tablespoon unsweetened cocoa powder
Pinch of salt

Place the half-and-half, chocolate chips, sugar, cocoa powder, and salt in a small saucepan; bring to a simmer over medium heat, stirring with a whisk until the chocolate melts and the mixture is smooth. Let it cool; pour into a covered jar and refrigerate until cold, about 2 hours. Makes about ⅔ cup.

Meanwhile, place the milk, chocolates, sugar, Marshmallow Creme, and salt in a small saucepan; bring to a simmer over medium heat, whisking constantly; the mixture will be frothy. Remove from the heat and whisk in the vanilla. Pour into heated mugs; stir in liqueur if desired, or add a cinnamon stick for stirring and top with marshmallows, if using.

Makes 1¼ cups or 2 servings

Superrich Coconut Cream Hot Chocolate

This is the après-ski drink I want when I have been playing hard outside in the snow. It is creamy and so full of coconut flavor from both the coconut milk and the cream of coconut mixer. The coconut flavored whipped cream on top is a must, too.

½ cup whole milk
½ cup well-stirred unsweetened coconut milk
2 tablespoons well-stirred canned cream of coconut, such as Coco Lopez
1¾ ounces semisweet chocolate, chopped
Pinch of salt
½ teaspoon pure vanilla extract
Coconut Whipped Cream (recipe follows)

Heat 2 mugs by filling them with very hot tap water; let the mugs stand until they feel warm to the touch, 1 to 2 minutes. Pour out the water.

Meanwhile, place the milk, coconut milk, and cream of coconut in a small saucepan; bring to a simmer over medium heat, stirring constantly until the sugar melts. Add the chocolate and salt; cook just until the chocolate melts, stirring until smooth. Remove from the heat and stir in the vanilla.

Pour into heated mugs; top with dollops of Coconut Whipped Cream.

Makes 2 servings

Coconut Whipped Cream

¼ cup cold heavy (whipping) cream

1 tablespoon well-stirred canned cream of coconut, such as Coco Lopez

2 teaspoons confectioners' sugar

Place the cream, cream of coconut, and the confectioners' sugar in a small, deep mixing bowl; beat at high speed with a handheld electric mixer until firm peaks form.

Makes ⅔ cup

~

Vanilla Chai White Hot Chocolate

My girlfriend and I tested this one early fall afternoon, sitting on the front porch swing while we enjoyed a quiet moment before she headed off to pick up her two-year-old son from "school." She said it was just the soothing cup she needed to ready—and steady— her state of mind. For me, it was a fragrant reminder that a season of creamy, sweet hot chocolate days were ahead and I was ready for them with this recipe.

I will also keep this in mind for a sophisticated dessert, with a shot of Cognac stirred into the mug.

> 1 cup whole milk
> One 2-inch piece vanilla bean
> 2 Chai-spice black tea bags
> 3 ounces fine-quality white chocolate, chopped
> Pinch of salt
> 2 tablespoons brandy, optional
> Cinnamon sticks, optional

Heat 2 mugs by filling them with very hot tap water; let the mugs stand until they feel warm to the touch, 1 to 2 minutes. Pour out the water.

Meanwhile, place the milk in a small, heavy saucepan. Split open the vanilla bean by slicing it lengthwise down one side using the tip of a small sharp knife. Use the tip of a table knife to scrape the seeds into the milk mixture. Add the tea bags; bring to a simmer over medium heat, stirring constantly. Cover, remove from the heat, and let stand 5 minutes. Remove the tea bags, pressing lightly on the bags to extract all the liquid.

Stir in the white chocolate and salt until the chocolate melts. Pour into heated mugs; pour 1 ounce of brandy into each mug, if desired. Garnish with cinnamon sticks, if desired.

Makes 2 servings

Variation

Vanilla White Hot Chocolate: For just Vanilla White Hot Chocolate, omit the tea bags.

Chocolate Raspberry Dessert Smoothies

You can dress these up with liqueur, or make them with extra milk instead for a non-alcoholic version. But either way, they are the perfect blend of raspberries and chocolate.

> 1½ cups frozen raspberries, thawed and undrained
> ½ cup whole milk
> 1½ cups frozen chocolate yogurt
> ¼ cup Homemade Chocolate Syrup (page 311)
> ¼ cup Chambord or other raspberry liqueur or to taste, optional

Chill 2 tall glasses.

Press the raspberries through a fine mesh sieve into a blender container, pressing hard on the solids to extract all the liquid. Add the milk, frozen yogurt, Homemade Chocolate Syrup, and liqueur, if using, to the blender container; process the mixture until smooth and thick. Pour into the chilled glasses.

Makes 2 servings

Malted Milk Chocolate Shakes

These were the darlings of malt shops and drugstore counters all over the country, thanks to a clever soda "jerk" in 1922 at Walgreen's in Chicago. Up until Ivar "Pop" Coulson invented the shake, malted milk drinks consisted of milk, chocolate milk, and a spoonful of malt powder. During a particularly hot day, "Pop" added scoops of ice cream and the malted milk shake shook up the soda fountain world. Good times, great shakes.

> 15 malted milk balls, such as Whoppers
> ⅔ cup cold whole milk
> 1 pint premium-quality vanilla bean ice cream
> 2 tablespoons malted milk powder
> 2 tablespoons Homemade Chocolate Syrup (page 311)
> 1 teaspoon pure vanilla extract

Chill two tall glasses.

Place ten malted milk balls in a heavy-duty plastic bag; crush with a rolling pin. Set them aside. Chop the remaining five malted milk balls, and set them aside for the tops of the shakes.

Place the milk, ice cream, malted milk powder, Homemade Chocolate Syrup, vanilla, and the crushed malted milk balls in a blender container. Process until it is thick and creamy, stopping the blender and pushing down on the ice cream as necessary. Pour the shake into the chilled glasses and sprinkle the tops with the chopped malted milk balls.

Makes 2 servings

Variation

White Chocolate Vanilla Malted Shakes: For vanilla purists, this version is a must. Substitute 2 tablespoons white chocolate cocoa mix, such a Ghiradelli Sweet Ground White Chocolate, for the Homemade Chocolate Syrup. And if you have it, substitute 1 teaspoon vanilla bean paste for the extract. Omit the malted milk balls.

Luscious Chocolate Peanut Butter Shakes

It does not get much better than this. My youngest daughter and I share these often on the deck when the weather is warm and we need a break. She calls it our "mother-daughter bonding time."

½ cup cold chocolate milk (not low-fat) or whole milk
1 pint chocolate ice cream
3 tablespoons creamy peanut butter
2 tablespoons Homemade Chocolate Syrup (page 311)
1 teaspoon pure vanilla extract
6 mini peanut butter cup candies, such as Reese's, unwrapped and
    finely chopped, or 1 small Butterfingers candy bar, finely chopped

Chill two tall glasses.

Place the milk, ice cream, peanut butter, Homemade Chocolate Syrup, and vanilla in a blender container; process until it is thick and creamy, stopping the blender and pressing down on the ice cream as necessary. Pour into the chilled glasses and sprinkle with the candy.

Makes 2 servings

For Chocolate Peanut Butter Banana Shakes Slice a small banana and arrange the slices in a single layer on a baking sheet. Freeze until they are solid, about

30 minutes. Add the frozen banana slices to the blender along with the milk, ice cream, peanut butter, Homemade Chocolate Syrup, and vanilla extract, reducing the ice cream amount to 2 cups.

Makes 2 servings

❦

Alisia's Chocolate Martini

My stepdaughter's great friend is one-half of a super-chef couple here in Asheville. Alisia Parrott offered up her martini recipe for this book and I was thrilled; I have tasted a few of her dessert creations and I knew whatever drink she shook up would be innovative and fabulous.

> 1 ounce Godiva chocolate liqueur
> 1½ ounces Stoli Vanil or Absolut Vanilia (vanilla-flavored vodka)
> ½ ounce crème de cacao (light), or other liqueur flavor options (see below)

Rim the glass: Dip the edge into a small dish of chocolate syrup, crème de cacao, or water and roll the rim into a small dish of shaved chocolate to coat it.

Pour the Godiva liqueur into the bottom of the glass.

Pour the Stoli and crème de cacao into a martini shaker with ice. Shake and pour over the Godiva by using a spoon to allow the clear liquid to gently layer on top of the chocolate liqueur.

To garnish, Alisia places a single chocolate truffle in the bottom of the glass with a swizzle stick "handle" inserted in the truffle; it resembles a chocolate lollipop inverted in the glass.

Makes 1 serving

Variations

Instead of the crème de cacao, substitute ½ ounce

- Frangelico or another hazelnut liqueur: rim the glass with finely ground hazelnuts mixed with cocoa powder.

- Chambord: rim the glass with shaved chocolate and float a single raspberry in the drink.

- Cointreau: rim the glass with Homemade Chocolate Syrup (page 311) and garnish with a thin orange twist.

∽

ACKNOWLEDGMENTS

❧

I developed and tested the recipes in this book as I moved to a different state with my nine-year-old daughter and married my high school sweetheart. Baking brownies was the balm that soothed new school jitters for Eleni. Offering trays of assorted chocolate cakes and pies made us friendly with the neighbors. And testing tiny chocolate layer cakes helped my new husband, Lindsay Ayliffe, deal with the unpacked boxes. Thank you, little family, for your enthusiasm and support.

Heartfelt thanks to my agent, Patricia Moosbrugger, for loving the concept of baking in small batches and helping promote this niche.

Thanks to Kathleen Gilligan, my editor at Thomas Dunne, for her excitement about this project. Thanks to her, there are color photos in the book that illustrate how beautiful small-batch desserts can be. And I appreciate the many ways copy editor Leah Stewart and production editor Jane Liddle made this book so much more clear to read.

These mouthwatering photos are the work of photographer Sandra Stambaugh. She lives and works in Asheville, North Carolina, my new hometown, and I was a lucky author to find such a talented food photographer in this city. Thank you, Sandi, for putting in the extra time and effort to get the shots just right and make my desserts look gorgeous.

Jennifer Thomas, local pastry chef and friend, helped out with testing a few cookies while I was in rush stages of completion. These recipes couldn't have been put into better hands. Thanks for pitching in, Jen.

As always, thanks to Martha Johnston for her faithful encouragement and sage advice.

INDEX

Smoothies
    chocolate raspberry dessert, 316
Snickers bar
    in Chocolate Caramel-Swirled Peanut Giants,
        138–39
    in Dulce de Leche Brownies, 170
S'Mores Brownies, 173–74
Soufflé(s)
    cakes, chocolate, 38–39
    chocolate cookie chip, 197–98
    chocolate Earl Grey tea, 199–201
    chocolate peanut, with peanut butter custard
        sauce, 194–96
    serving tips, 196
Sour cream, storing, 12
Sour Cream Chocolate Ganache, 18
Southern Living Cooking Schools, 290
Southern Living magazine, 140
Southern Pecan and Chocolate Chip Pies, 288–89
Spatulas, rubber, 7
Spices, storing, 12
Stars, chocolate, 30
Strawberry Chocolate Tarts, 98–99
Strawberry Crème Anglaise, 87
Strawberry White Chocolate Icing, 26–27
Streusel, white chocolate raspberry coconut,
        bars, 165–66
Stuckey's, 175
Sugar cookies, chocolate, 302–304
Superrich Coconut Cream Hot Chocolate, 312–13
Sugar Syrup, 220
Sweetened flaked coconut, 13
Syrup
    chocolate, homemade, 311
    sugar, 220

Talisker Crème Anglaise, 80
Talisker Fudge Tarts with Hazelnut Cookie
        Crusts, 78–79

Tarts. See also Pies
    caramel nut, bittersweet, 259–60
    chocolate-covered cherry almond, 83–84
    chocolate cranberry truffle, 285–87
    chocolate derby pecan, 290–91
    chocolate lavender cream, 88–89
    chocolate orange truffle, 281–82
    chocolate pineapple custard, 91–92
    mocha chocolate pudding, 93–95
    peanut butter fudge, 96–97
    salted chocolate caramel nut, 76–77
    strawberry chocolate, 98–99
    truffle, bittersweet, with salted pistachio
        brittle, 283–84
Tassies, chocolate coconut pecan, 140–41
Tea drinks
    Earl Grey, chocolate, soufflés, 199–201
    Vanilla Chai White Hot Chocolate, 314–15
Tea loaf, chocolate, 219–20
Texas Sheet Cake, 32–34
Thick Chocolate Glaze, 71
Thumbprints, chocolate caramel, 152–53
Toasting hazelnuts, 156
Toblerone chocolate bar, in Chocolate Almond
        Candy Shortbread, 179–80
Toffee
    cashew, crunch chocolate torte, 50–52
    chocolate, biscotti, 183–84
Top-Loaded Brownies, 170
Toppings for cheesecakes, 105–106
    Candy Cane Cheesecakes, 106
    Jewel Boxes, 105–106
    Shimmering Apricot Glaze, 105
    White and Chocolate Swirled Ganache
        Topping, 105
Torte
    cashew toffee crunch chocolate, 50–52
    truffle, chocoholic's, 35–37
Triple chocolate, oatmeal chippers, giant, 146–47